find your Style
and Knit it too

by Sharon Turner

BICENTENNIAL
1807
WILEY
2007
BICENTENNIAL

Wiley Publishing, Inc.

Find Your Style and Knit It Too

Copyright © 2008 by Wiley Publishing, Inc., Hoboken, New Jersey. All rights reserved.

Published by Wiley Publishing, Inc., Hoboken, New Jersey

For general information on our other products and services or to obtain technical support please contact our Customer Care Department within the U.S. at (800) 762-2974, outside the U.S. at (317) 572-3993 or fax (317) 572-4002.

Wiley also publishes its books in a variety of electronic formats. Some content that appears in print may not be available in electronic books. For more information about Wiley products, please visit our web site at www.wiley.com.

Library of Congress Cataloging-in-Publication Data:
Turner, Sharon, 1962–
  Find your style and knit it too / by Sharon Turner.
     p. cm.
  ISBN-13: 978-0-470-13987-5
  ISBN-10: 0-470-13987-0
  1. Knitting. I. Title.
  TT820.T876 2007
  746.43'2—dc22

                          2007028419

Printed in the United States of America

10 9 8 7 6 5 4 3 2 1

Book production by Wiley Publishing, Inc., Composition Services

Credits

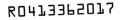

Acquisitions Editor
Roxane Cerda

Project Editor
Kitty Wilson Jarrett

Technical Editor
Alexandra Virgiel

Editorial Manager
Christina Stambaugh

Publisher
Cindy Kitchel

Vice President and Executive Publisher
Kathy Nebenhaus

Interior Design
Erin Zeltner
Kathie Rickard

Cover Design
Cynthia Frenette

Photography
Jodi Bratch

Graphics Specialists
Joni Burns
Laura Campbell

For my daughters, Isabel, Matilda, and Phoebe, who have such great style

About the Author

Sharon Turner designs knitwear and publishes a line of knitting patterns called Monkeysuits. She is the author of *Monkeysuits: Sweaters and More to Knit for Kids*, *Teach Yourself Visually Knitting*, *Teach Yourself Visually Knitting Design*, and *Knitting Visual Quick Tips*. She lives in Brooklyn, New York, with her husband and three daughters.

Acknowledgments

This fun project has been a collaborative endeavor from the get-go. Roxane Cerda at Wiley and my wonderful agent, Marilyn Allen, helped brainstorm the first idea for this book into what it is now. Thanks again to Roxane Cerda and Cindy Kitchel for taking on the project and for being so much fun to work with. Grateful acknowledgment also goes out to photographer Jodi Bratch and the bright and beautiful models—Brianna, Chandler, McKenzie, Katie, Laura, Hannah, Emily, Laryn, Mary, and Taylor (and their families) for doing such a super job showing off the knits; to Chris Stambaugh and the design team at Wiley for pulling it all together and for the fun book design, inside and out; and to Alexandra Virgiel for her eagle-eyed technical expertise.

Joining forces with contributing designers Kitty Jarrett, Alison Stewart-Guinee, Jill Draper, Heather Brack, Claudine Monique, and Shannon Okey has been invigorating and inspiring. Thank you all for jumping in with such enthusiasm—and with such amazing projects. Hugs to editor Kitty Jarrett, who has become my e-mail friend, and whose way with words and knitting know-how are invaluable. (Let's do another one!)

My husband, Mark, and my daughters Isabel and Matilda contributed by always patiently answering my annoying questions regarding style and color. My youngest daughter, Phoebe, keeps us all laughing—let's just hope that continues through *her* teen years.

Grateful acknowledgment goes to the following yarn suppliers for their generosity in providing yarn for this book's projects:

Cascade Yarns (supplier of Cascade and Di.Ve' yarns), www.cascadeyarns.com

elann.com (Internet retail supplier of elann.com Peruvian Collection and much more), www.elann.com

Lion Brand Yarns, www.lionbrand.com

Louet North America, www.louet.com

Muench Yarns (supplier of Muench and GGH yarns), www.muenchyarns.com

South West Trading Company, www.soysilk.com

The publisher would also like to thank Todd Robinson and LUNA music for graciously hosting a photo shoot. LUNA music can be found at www.lunamusic.net.

Table of Contents

Introduction

There are all kinds of knitters, and knitting has something fun to offer all kinds of people: You can use it to play with color, texture, pattern, and fashion—even math! Plus, it's relaxing and makes you feel good. So whether you're new to knitting or not, jump into this book, take a few lessons, and find out what kind of knitter *you* are. No matter what kind of knitter you are, or what style you wear, knitting basics are pretty much the same for everyone. Rows and rows of little loops of yarn linked together form knit fabrics of all types. People have been knitting for centuries; the difference between then and now is *you* get to do it for fun, whereas in olden days, people had to knit out of necessity. (Though I'm sure they must have enjoyed it—who wouldn't?)

Part 1 of this book tells you all you need to know to choose materials and learn how to knit. If you already know how to knit, you can polish your skills—there's always more to discover! You'll learn about yarn, needles, and the other important tools. The essential techniques of casting on, knitting, purling, and binding off are all covered, accompanied by helpful illustrations. Once you master the basics, you can move on to trying out your new knits and purls to form interesting stitch patterns. What if you make a mistake? No worries; you'll learn how to fix them here. In this part, you'll also learn how to knit new shapes by increasing and decreasing. When you get really good at that, you can start making lace, cables, and color patterns in your knitting—it's not as hard as you think. You can also try knitting in circles—or *in the round*—to create socks, leg warmers, seamless hats, and mittens. Finally, the end of this part includes lots of useful information about finishing your knitting—making buttonholes, knitting pockets, sewing seams, and adding pompoms and embroidery.

After you learn how to knit, or improve the skills you already have, you can find your style in Part 2 and knit away. Quite a few of the projects are quick and small—providing instant gratification and minimal frustration without sacrificing style. Whether you're a beginner or a more experienced knitter, a punk or a preppy, you'll find a whole bunch of fun knitting projects in this part of the book—from quick and easy things for impatient types to more involved projects for more of a challenge. You can skip straight to your particular style type(s), or, if you refuse to be categorized, flip through the pages and see what you like. There's something for everyone. (If you're a grunge lover, check out the bonus chapter at www.wiley.com/go/findyourstyle, where you'll find patterns for legwarmers and a matching hat as well as a pair of wrist warmers.)

And don't think you have to limit yourself to one or two styles. Suggestions for how to alter projects to suit different tastes accompany many of the designs.

part 1

knitting
know-how

1. If you were yarn, you would be:
   a. A big ball of super-bulky.
   b. Something hairy with glitter in it.
   c. A machine-washable yarn in a primary color.
   d. I can't choose—I love all kinds of yarn.

2. It's time to start a new knitting project! You:
   a. Look for something that will be quick—in the fattest yarn with the biggest needles.
   b. Choose a pattern for an elegant accessory, like a bag or wrap.
   c. Don't look for a pattern since you probably won't understand it. You just want to make something in garter stitch because that's what you know how to do.
   d. Search for something that looks fun—but also a little challenging—in a yarn that will suit the project best.

3. You like to:
   a. Start new projects and finish them in a hurry. If the project doesn't move along quickly, you'll never finish it at all.
   b. Knit fashionable accessories, like scarves, wristbands, hand warmers, and little bags.
   c. Knit to relax—it doesn't really matter what it turns out like. It's the knitting that's the fun part.
   d. Knit everything—anytime, anywhere. Knitting is your passion, and you're determined to learn all the tricks.

4. Your favorite needles are:
   a. The jumbo ones for fat yarns or the metal ones that help you knit faster.
   b. The pretty ones with the decorative knobs on top.
   c. The least expensive needles you can buy.
   d. Short bamboo needles for scarves, metal circular needles for big projects, wooden double-pointed needles for hats . . . oh, I don't know, I like them all!

5. When it comes to knitting patterns, you like:
   a. Simple, easy-to-read patterns, with lots of pictures.
   b. The latest patterns in the best-selling knitting magazines.
   c. To knit without a pattern.
   d. To consult books, magazines, yarn manufacturers' publications—you name it.

if you answered:

Mostly a's: Slow down—it's not a race! You love to knit, but your attention span for it is limited, and you want results fast. Stick to the big needles and fat yarn if that's what you love, but try to work in a few new techniques and take on a bigger project now and then. Don't be scared off by less–than–bulky yarns: Small projects in thinner yarns can go quickly, too!

Mostly b's: You love to dress up, and you love things that sparkle—baubles, ornaments, and frills are your thing. Even your knitting needles are dressed up! You should try knitting cables and lace and learn some new knitted embel–lishments and trimming techniques. Remember, however, that not everyone likes glittery scarves and chapeaux; if you want to give your boy–friend or family members knitted gifts, it might be a good idea to acquaint yourself with some traditional worsted–weight wool.

Mostly c's: Hmm . . . you like to knit, but you're not too into wearable results or all the cool stuff that goes with the hobby—yet. It sounds like you need a little nudge to further your skills, or knitting might get boring for you pretty soon. Don't be afraid to purl! It's just like knitting, only you do it on the front of the needles instead of at the back. Learn a new technique now and then. Remember how proud you were when you knit your first row?

Mostly d's: You're a knitting addict! When you walk into a yarn shop, you have to remind yourself to stay calm and to take a deep breath. You love all the colors, fibers, and textures; it's all so stimulating. You love to pore over the latest knitting publications and dream about future projects. You probably have quite a stash of yarn under your bed already. You take on ambitious projects and are happy to learn new techniques and put them to use. Just remember to take it slow and don't stock up on too many future projects: Fashions change, and you do have the rest of your life to knit!

Chapter 1
get set!

Now that you have this book, you're ready to learn how to knit, but do you have everything else you need to start knitting? You need yarn, needles, and a few little tools to begin with. After you've been knitting for a while, you'll naturally accumulate more yarn—LOTS more yarn, if you love knitting— plus more needles and accessories, so don't buy too much at first. What kind of yarn should you get? And what size and type of needles do you want? This chapter tells you all you need to know to make the right choices.

it's all about yarn

One of the most fun parts of knitting is choosing yarn. You may feel overwhelmed when you set out to buy yarn for your first project. Knitting yarns come in so many fibers, weights, textures, and colors that it can be confusing. Take a deep breath, read on, and you'll get a better idea of what to look for.

natural fibers

Natural fibers come from animals and plants. Wool, alpaca, mohair, cashmere, and angora are spun from animal fibers, and they're really warm to wear—and fun to knit with. Certain wools, like Shetland wool, can be scratchy; some, like merino, are nice and soft. Be sure to hold a ball of yarn against your skin to see if you would want to wear something made out of it. It would be a bummer to spend weeks knitting a scarf that is too itchy to wear.

Alpaca is a soft fiber that knits to a flexible, soft fabric. Mohair is hairier than wool, and things knit in mohair–only yarns have a fuzzy halo. So do things made out of angora, which is softer than mohair and comes from angora rabbits. Cashmere comes from goats—it is one of the softest yarns, but it's very expensive. Silk, produced by silkworms, is warm but not as stretchy as wool.

btw: Don't worry; bunnies, sheep, and goats don't get killed for their hair or wool. Angora is harvested by combing the rabbits a couple times a year. Sheep get haircuts: Their wool is shorn once or twice a year.

Cotton and linen yarns—also not as springy as wool—are made from plants, and they're good for things you wear in the summer or in a warm climate. They are also great for bags and accessories.

unnatural fibers

There are a number of synthetic, human-made fibers, including acrylic, nylon, and polyester. These yarns are sometimes less expensive than natural fibers, and many are machine washable. In olden days, acrylic yarn was horrible, rough, scratchy stuff; now you can find some highly respectable acrylics. Nylon is often used to reinforce wool, like for sock yarns, but there are also 100% nylon furry yarns that are downy soft and almost weightless.

fiber blends

Spinning two or more fibers together into one yarn makes a *blend*. The combinations are infinite: Even yarns containing the same fibers can be vastly different due to the amount of each fiber in the blend. For example, a wool/mohair blend that has 85% wool and 15% mohair will be slightly hairy, while combining the same two fibers 50–50 results in a totally different yarn. Sometimes fibers are blended to produce a less expensive yarn or a machine-washable yarn. Mixing one fiber with another can change the undesirable aspects of a fiber for the better. For instance, cotton can gain body and springiness by being combined with acrylic; combining wool with alpaca, angora, or cashmere can soften it.

yarn textures and colors

In addition to coming in different fibers and weights, yarn also comes in a zillion different textures, colors, and color blends. Furry, bumpy, metallic, and hairy yarns are called *novelty yarns*. These yarns are fun for edgings and dressy stuff, and they can be doubled up with another yarn to add some pizzazz. Even non-novelty yarns vary in texture from one to the next, depending on fiber content and how they're spun. You'll also see lots of colorful yarns—yarns that come in variegated color mixes or tweeds.

You will no doubt be tempted to buy some of these fun and fuzzy or rainbow-colored yarns. But if you're a beginner, don't do it! You can't learn how to knit with this stuff: It's too difficult to see the stitches beneath all that texture or amid that riot of color, and knitting with novelty yarns evenly takes some skill and practice. So for now, stick with a nice smooth traditionally spun yarn, preferably good old 100% wool, in a light to medium shade (it's hard to see the stitches in too-dark colors) of your favorite color.

balls, skeins, and hanks

Ball, *skein*, and *hank* are the names of the different forms yarn comes in when you buy it. A ball is—you guessed it—round. Skeins can be a few different shapes, sometimes long and cylindrical with a label wrapped around the middle, and sometimes shaped like an oblong ball. A hank is different from these two because it's not machine-wound into a ready-to-use form. It looks kind of like a twisted cruller, and you have to untwist it and wind it into a ball yourself. Sometimes a nice yarn shop will wind a hank into a ball for you using a yarn swift—if you're buying the hank from that shop, of course. If you see a yarn swift, a big contraption that looks like an umbrella skeleton mounted onto a table in the store, ask if they'll wind your hank into a ball. It will be well worth it in the end, since rolling it into a ball can take quite some time (and be frustrating, if it gets tangled).

btw: If you have to buy multiple hanks for a project, it's a good idea to wind all but one. This way, if you use less yarn than expected, you might be able to return the unused hank; most stores won't take back a hank that's been wound.

yarn weights

Yarn comes in many thicknesses, which are called *weights*—not to be confused with the actual weight, in ounces or grams, of the ball or skein. Yarn weight is labeled from thinnest to thickest as super fine, fine, light, medium, bulky, and super bulky. You use fat needles for bulky yarns and thin needles for fine yarns. Super–fine yarns are also called fingering, baby, lace–weight, and sock yarn. Fine yarns can be referred to as sport weight or baby. Light yarns include yarns called double–knitting (DK) and light worsted. Medium yarns are also described as worsted, Aran, or afghan yarn. Bulky generally refers to yarns labeled chunky or heavy worsted. Super–bulky yarns are usually called just that—super bulky. See the chart below for more information about yarn weight.

standard yarn weight system

Yarn Weight Category Name	Type of Yarns in Category	Knit Gauge Range* in Stockinette Stitch to 4 Inches	Recommended Needle Range, in US Size	Recommended Needle Range, in Metric Size
Super fine	Sock, fingering, baby, lace	27–32 stitches	1–3	2.25–3.25 mm
Fine	Sport, baby	23–26 stitches	3–5	3.25–3.75 mm
Light	DK, light worsted	21–24 stitches	5–7	3.75–4.5 mm
Medium	Worsted, afghan, Aran	16–20 stitches	7–9	4.5–5.5 mm
Bulky	Chunky, heavy worsted, bulky, craft, rug	12–15 stitches	9–11	5.5–8 mm
Super bulky	Super bulky	6–11 stitches	11 and larger	8 mm and larger

* The gauges listed are guidelines only; this table reflects the most commonly used gauges and needle sizes for specific yarn categories.

yarn substitutions

Chances are you'll want or need to substitute a differ-ent yarn than the one specified in a pattern. Either the yarn shop won't have the one you need, or you'll want a different fiber, or you'll want to spend less (or more) than the yarn in the pattern costs. The single most important thing to consider when subbing one yarn for another is the weight: If you want the pattern to come out the right shape and size, you need to get yarn that is the same weight and that knits to the same gauge. Remember that weight means thickness here, not the weight of the ball.

See the picture of the little knit squares called *swatches*? They were knit from yarns of different weights, using the same number of stitches; as you can see, they're completely different sizes. That's why knitting a gauge swatch is so important when you start a project. If you substitute a yarn with a different gauge, you can end up with a doll–sized hat instead of one that fits you. (For more about gauge, see page 37.) A fun thing to do is combine two or more different yarns to get the right thickness—you create your own new yarn that way! Once you find yarn that is the correct weight, you need to check how many yards the pattern says you need and buy the same number of yards in the new yarn. See the next section for more on yarn yardage.

reading a yarn label

Most yarns come with a label, sometimes called a *ball band*, on them. It may seem really boring, but you need to know what all that tiny type on your yarn label means. You wouldn't want to skip read‑ing the label and end up with a sweater that's so small you can't get it over your head because the gauge is wrong, or miss the care instructions on the label and turn your cashmere scarf into a felted potholder. So be sure to read the ball band and save it for later, with a little bit of the yarn it came with.

btw: To keep track of the details of your knitting adven‑tures, try starting a scrapbook or diary. You can start by saving the ball band and bits of yarn. Then you can include your stitch pattern swatch, notes about the pat‑tern, what size you knit, techniques you used or learned—even what was happening in your life when you knit the project.

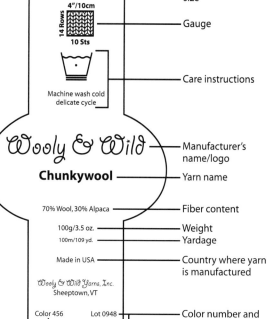

The largest words on the ball band are usually the yarn manufacturer's name/logo and the name of the particular yarn. Also included is the fiber content of the yarn. The label lists the weight of the ball and the *yardage*, which is the length of yarn in the ball. In addition, you'll see a color number or name, along with a dye lot number. Yarn gets dyed in big batches, called *lots*, and each lot is slightly different from the next. So it's important to buy yarn for one project all from the same dye lot, or you'll end up with a funny‑looking line on your sweater where the two lots meet. It doesn't usually look good. On the other hand, if you use no‑dye‑lot yarn, you don't have to worry about this problem at all. No‑dye‑lot yarn is an inexpensive acrylic yarn that you can buy at the big craft supply chain stores.

Somewhere on the label, you'll see what size knitting needles the manufacturer recommends for the yarn, along with the suggested gauge for that yarn on those needles. Gauge on a yarn label is simply how many stitches and rows it takes to get a 4‑inch or (10 cm) square with that yarn on the recommended needle. This starts to get kind of mathematical, but it's *very* important, so read more about gauge on p. 37.

Finally, the care instructions for the yarn usually appear as symbols like the ones you see on cloth-ing labels. You can use this chart to see what the symbols mean.

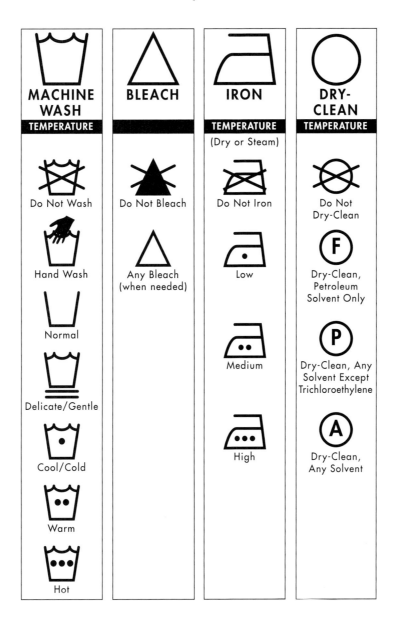

the skinny on knitting needles

Knitting needles come in many shapes and sizes, and they are made out of different materials. You can get fat needles, skinny needles, straight needles, single-pointed needles, double-pointed needles, or circular needles—and they can be made of wood, metal, bamboo, or plastic. In case you're having a hard time figuring out what kind to get, here's a little help.

needle materials

Most knitting needles come in metal, plastic, wood, or bamboo. Metal needles are slippery, so the yarn slides easily along them. This can be a good thing if you want to go fast, but it can be a bad thing if you're a beginner and your stitches keep sliding off and unraveling. Plastic needles are lightweight and inexpensive. They can bend, particularly if exposed to heat, so don't leave them near a radiator. Wood needles are very pretty and are usually more expensive than metal or plastic. Bamboo needles are lighter and tend to be less expensive than wood needles. Bamboo is an excellent choice for beginners because the surface is smooth but not slippery, so it slows the yarn down and keeps stitches from sliding off the needle.

needle shapes

Knitting needles come in three shapes: straight, double-pointed, and circular. Straight needles, a.k.a. single-pointed needles, are the ones most commonly used. They're sold in pairs and have a point on one end and a knob on the other. They come in a couple different lengths: 10 inches for small stuff like scarves and baby things, and 14 inches for sweaters and larger items. Double-pointed needles are sold in sets of four or five, and they have a point on each end. They're good for knitting tubular things like socks, mittens, and hats. Circular needles are sold singly. They have two points connected by a nylon cord, and they come in many lengths and materials. They're good for large tubular items like pullovers and skirts; but you can also use them for knitting big, flat things like blankets, sweaters, and shawls. They hold a large number of stitches easily and are more portable than straight needles. Also, if you're knitting in close quarters, like on an airplane or on the subway, circulars are best because you won't keep elbowing and jabbing your neighbor.

needle sizes

Needle sizing can be very confusing. Just one needle can have three numbers indicating the size. The most important measurement is the diameter, or the thickness, of the needle. The diameter is measured in millimeters, and the size for this is the number followed by "mm." There is also a US size system that starts with 0 for the thinnest and ends with 50 for the thickest—you'll learn what US size equals which "mm" as you knit more and more. Watch out if you're knitting from Canadian or British instructions: They may use a different numbering system. And if you buy needles online, especially in an online auction, you might get needles produced somewhere that uses a different numbering system. That's why it's always best to buy needles based on the diameter in millimeters than on the numbering system.

The needle size is listed on the package, but what if you lose the package? Most straight needles have the size imprinted on the knob at the end or stamped into the wood or bamboo near the end. For circular needles, the size is trickier to find. It's sometimes engraved into or printed on the metal at the base of the tip, or if not there, it may be printed on the nylon cord between the tips. If your needles don't show a size, you can use a needle gauge (see page 10) to measure the diameter. A needle package also lists the length in inches; remember that short needles are good for small things, and long needles are best for big things.

So, now that you know how to find the needle's size, it's time to learn why this little diameter number is so important. The diameter of the needle determines the size of the stitches and therefore affects the gauge. *Gauge* is the number of stitches and rows knit per inch. All knitting patterns are written based on a certain gauge. For example, a scarf that is 6 inches wide, knit at a gauge of 5 stitches per inch, will require 30 stitches on the needles. (After the knitting and purling how–to sections, there is an in–depth lesson on gauge. Check out page 37.) Yarn labels usually list a recommended gauge and needle size. So if you're just starting out, buy the needles recommended on the ball band. Don't try knitting fat yarn on skinny needles, or you'll hate knitting so much that you'll give up after one row. Here's a handy chart that lists the US sizes and their corresponding measurements, in millimeters.

knitting needle sizes

Metric (mm)	US Size
2.0 mm	0
2.25 mm–2.5 mm	1
2.75 mm	2
3.25 mm	3
3.5 mm	4
3.75 mm	5
4.0 mm	6
4.5 mm	7
5.0 mm	8
5.5 mm	9
6.0 mm	10
6.5 mm or 7 mm*	$10^1/_2$
7.0 mm*	$10^3/_4$
8.0 mm	11
9.0 mm	13
10.0 mm	15
12.0 mm–12.75 mm	17
15.0 mm–16.0 mm	19
19.0 mm	35
25.0 mm	50

* Needle manufacturers can't seem to agree on the size of US $10^1/_2$ needles. Some produce $10^1/_2$ needles that are 6.5 mm, and some make theirs 7.0 mm. Some manufacturers even call their 7.0 mm needles US $10^3/_4$.

accessorize

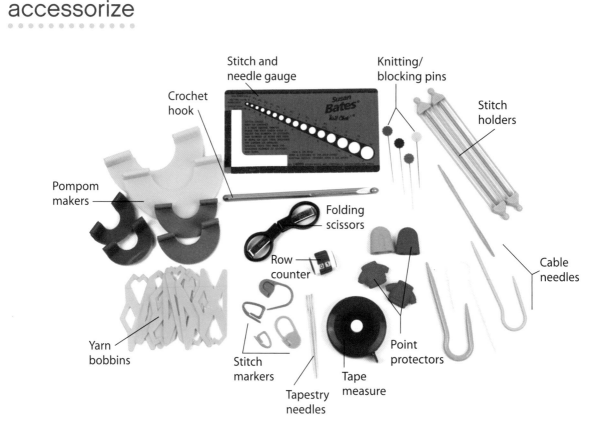

Stitch and needle gauge

Knitting/blocking pins

Crochet hook

Stitch holders

Pompom makers

Folding scissors

Cable needles

Row counter

Yarn bobbins

Point protectors

Stitch markers

Tape measure

Tapestry needles

In addition to yarn and needles, you need to get a few accessories to keep in your knitting bag at all times. Oh, right—first things first. You need a knitting bag. It can be a little shopping bag from your favorite store, or it can be something more permanent if you're really committed. Look around in your closet or under your bed for a bag that is roomy, has a pocket or a few pockets, and stands open. Canvas tote bags are great. (As you get going, you'll probably acquire a lot of knitting bags. Different size projects require different size bags, right? Most knit-a-holics are bag-a-holics, too.) Following are a few lists of accessories to put in your bag alongside your yarn and needles. Only the things in the first category are essential; the rest you will accumulate over time.

btw: Avoid using bags that have Velcro closures as knitting bags. Yarn—or even worse, your knitting project—can get snagged and damaged on those little loops.

essential accessories

- Tape measure for measuring your knitted pieces (the retractable ones are best)
- Small pair of scissors (folding scissors don't poke into your knitting or bag)
- Stitch and needle gauge to measure gauge and needle diameter
- Tapestry needles for sewing seams and weaving in ends
- Crochet hook for fixing dropped stitches
- Point protectors to prevent your knitting from slipping off the needles
- Row counter to keep track of how many rows you have worked
- Stitch holders for holding stitches to be worked later (you can use a strand of scrap yarn in a pinch)
- Plastic-headed, rustproof knitting pins to fasten knitted pieces together before sewing

useful accessories

- Stitch markers for marking a point in knitting where an increase, a decrease, or a pattern change occurs
- Cable needles for holding stitches to the front or back when making knit cables
- Yarn bobbins for holding small quantities of yarn in color knitting
- Pompom maker for making perfectly round, full pompoms

Chapter 2

now you're ready to knit

Knitting is made up of rows and rows of little loops called *stitches*. This chapter shows you how to get those first stitches on the needles and then how to knit and purl them in a couple of different ways.

Once you get knitting and purling down, the sky's the limit! In this chapter, you'll also learn how to join a new ball of yarn, how to get the stitches off the needles properly, and how to weave in the loose ends so that your finished piece of knitting is something you can feel proud of.

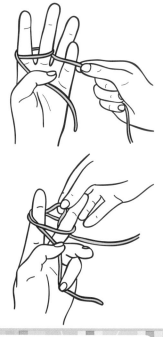

Now is the time to get out your yarn and needles. Remember, learning a new skill takes patience, so give it a little time.

cast on!

Casting on is what you do to get a foundation row of stitches on your needle so that you have something to knit. There are quite a few different cast-ons; here are a couple good ones to get you started.

the slipknot

All of the cast-on methods here begin with a slipknot. You have probably made a slipknot before. In knitting, it's the very first stitch you put on your needle. Here's how to do it:

1 Holding a 6-inch tail of the yarn against your palm, pulling from the ball yarn, wrap the yarn around your forefinger and middle finger twice, as shown.

2 Pull the yarn coming from the ball (this is called the *working yarn*) through the yarn wrapped around your fingers, forming a loop.

3 Insert the tip of one of your needles into the loop and pull the ends to secure it onto the needle. You have just put your first stitch—the slipknot—on the needle!

backward-loop cast-on

This is the quickest and easiest cast-on, so it's good for beginners. Use this to get some stitches on your needle to learn and practice, but use one of the other two cast-ons for projects that you're going to finish; this one doesn't create the neatest edge. The backward-loop cast-on is useful to know, however, because you can use it to make buttonholes or add stitches to your knitting. (But don't worry about that now!) Here's how you do it:

1 Holding the needle with the slipknot on it in your right hand and the working yarn in your left, make a loop, as shown, with the working yarn.

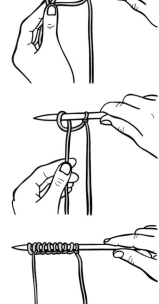

2 Place the loop onto the needle and pull on the working yarn to tighten it. You have cast on 1 stitch! There should now be 2 stitches on your needle—the slipknot and the cast-on stitch.

3 Repeat steps 1 and 2 until you have the correct number of stitches on your needle.

long-tail cast-on

Don't be scared off by this cast-on. It's one of the best all-around methods, and it really isn't as complicated as it looks. Have you ever done the farmer's pants or witch's broom in cat's cradle? If you can do that—or any other cat's cradle for that matter—learning this should be a breeze. This cast-on makes a neat and elastic edge. Here's how you do it:

1 Put a slipknot on your needle, leaving a tail that equals about 1 inch per stitch you're casting on, plus a few more inches. (For example, if you're casting on 12 stitches, leave a tail that's about 15 inches long.) You should have 2 strands hanging from your slipknot: the tail and the yarn attached to the ball. Hold this needle in your right hand.

2 With your left hand, part the 2 strands with your thumb and forefinger so that the tail end is draped over the outside of your thumb and the ball end is draped over the outside of your forefinger. Grasp the yarn ends to your palm with your pinky and ring finger.

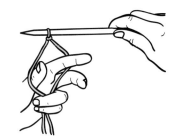

3 Lower the needle to make a V and to form loops around your thumb and forefinger. Hold the slipknot onto the needle with your right forefinger so it doesn't slide off.

4 Insert the needle up and under the outside of the thumb loop as shown.

5 Move the needle to the right and use it to reach over and grab the yarn from the near side of the forefinger loop (a); pull it down through the thumb loop (b).

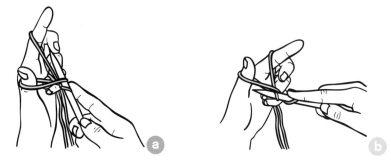

6 Drop the thumb loop and pull the tail to tighten the stitch securely on the needle. You have cast on 1 stitch! There should be 2 stitches on your needle—the slipknot and the cast-on stitch.

7 Repeat steps 2–6 until you have the correct number of stitches on your needle.

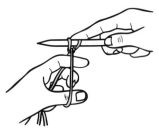

get comfy holding needles and yarn

If you watched a roomful of knitters, you'd see them all holding the needles and yarn in different ways. Some hold the yarn in their right hand, called the English method—most Americans knit this way—while others hold yarn in their left hand, called the Continental method. Different knitters wind the yarn around their left or right hand differently as well. What's most important is to find the style that feels relaxed and comfortable for you.

At first you'll feel awkward trying to hold the needles and the yarn all at the same time. Just like with any other new skill, practice leads to familiarity. Here are a few pointers on holding yarn and needles using both English and Continental styles.

english style

Knitting English style means holding and working the yarn in your right hand, but you don't have to be right-handed to knit this way. Many knitters wind the yarn around their hand and fingers so that the yarn doesn't feel loose and out of control. Some position the yarn as described below; this is the standard method you see described in books:

1. Holding the needle with the cast-on stitches on it in your left hand, wind the working yarn (the yarn coming from the ball) in a loop around your pinky, under your two middle fingers, and over the forefinger of your right hand.
2. Hold the empty needle—this is called the *working needle*—in your right hand while keeping the working yarn wound through your fingers to keep the tension even.

btw: Don't think that you have to do it this way if it's not comfortable. You should do what feels best for you: Try winding the yarn around your entire hand to keep it somewhat taut, or try looping it around the tip of your forefinger only. If none of these are comfortable, don't wind it around anything: Just grasp it between the thumb and forefinger of your right hand when you're knitting or purling a stitch.

continental style

Knitting Continental style means you hold and control the yarn with your left hand. Again, you don't have to be left-handed to choose this method. Here's how it works:

1. Holding the needle with the cast-on stitches on it in your right hand, wind the working yarn around the back of your hand, under your pinky and two middle fingers, and over the forefinger of your left hand.
2. Take the needle with the stitches on it back into your left hand, keeping the working yarn wound through your fingers to keep the yarn tension even, and hold the empty needle—this is called the *working needle*—in your right hand.

btw: The technique shown here for holding the yarn is just a suggestion. If this mode feels too loose or too awkward, try wrapping the yarn around your palm instead. The goal is to be comfortable and to have the yarn flow easily through your fingers.

knit stitches two ways

Finally! You can actually try knitting now. It's a good idea to start with a small number of stitches on your needle, say 15 to 20, so that you don't get lost and confused. Plus, you'll finish your first row sooner!

First, check to be sure your stitches aren't twisted and spiraling around your needle. Line up the knotted ends all in a row. Hold the working yarn at the back, behind the needles, to knit.

knit: english style

If you followed the instructions for holding the yarn in your right hand, English style, this is the knitting lesson for you. Get your needles and yarn positioned as described previously, or in a way that works for you. Here's how you knit English style:

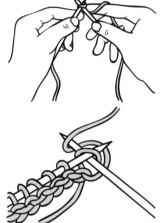

1 Holding the working yarn in back of both needles, insert the right needle into the front of the first stitch on the left needle, so that the needles form an X, with the right needle tip behind the left needle tip.

2 Holding the crossed needles between your left thumb and forefinger, wrap the working yarn around the right needle from back to front and then bring it down between the two needles.

3 Pull the tip of the right needle to the front, carrying the new loop of yarn you just wrapped around it in step 2 through the cast-on stitch (a), and push the shaft of the right needle against the front of the shaft of the left needle to slide the cast-on stitch up and off the left needle tip (b). You now have 1 stitch on your right needle—your first knit stitch!

4 Repeat steps 1–3 for each remaining cast-on stitch, until all of the new knit stitches are on the right needle. When you have done that, you have knit 1 row.

5 Switch the needle with the stitches on it to your left hand and repeat steps 1–4 for each row.

knit: continental style

If you followed the instructions for holding the yarn in your left hand, Continental style, this is the knitting lesson for you. Get your needles and yarn positioned comfortably as described previously, or in a way that works for you. Here's how you knit Continental style:

1 Holding the working yarn in back of both needles, insert the right needle into the front of the first stitch on the left needle, so that the needles form an X, with the right needle tip behind the left needle tip.

2 Use your left forefinger to wrap the working yarn around the right needle from front to back.

note: This is a small, quick motion of the left forefinger. You can help it along by grabbing the yarn with the right needle at the same time.

3 Pull the tip of the right needle to the front, carrying the new loop of yarn you just wrapped around it in step 2 through the cast-on stitch (a), and push the shaft of the right needle against the front of the shaft of the left needle to slide the cast-on stitch up and off the left needle tip (b). You now have 1 stitch on your right needle—your first knit stitch!

4 Repeat steps 1–3 for each remaining cast-on stitch, until all of the new knit stitches are on the right needle. When you have done that, you have knit 1 row.

5 Switch the needle with the stitches on it to your left hand and repeat steps 1–4 for each row.

If you're enjoying knitting and don't want to learn how to purl yet, then by all means keep on knitting. Knitting every row is called *garter stitch*—doesn't that sound important? So knit every row and make a little square, or keep going until it's a long enough rectangle to fold into a little purse. Keep going for a *really* long time, and you'll have a scarf. Then, to get your first project off the needles neatly and safely, skip ahead to "Bind Off Stitches" on page 20.

purl stitches two ways

Don't be afraid of purling—it's really just like knitting, but the opposite: The right needle starts out in the front and completes the stitch in the back. Learning how to purl opens up a whole world of possibilities. First, you can work in *stockinette stitch*, which is made by knitting a row, then purling a row, and so on. Most knitting is stockinette stitch. Ribbing and seed stitch are made up of knits and purls alternating in the same row. You'll have lots more fun—and lots more options—after you learn how to purl.

purl: english style

If you're holding the working yarn in your right hand to knit, then this is the lesson for you. Get your yarn and needles poised as you would to knit and then follow these steps:

1 Holding the working yarn in front of both needles, insert the right needle into the front of the first stitch on the left needle, from back to front (that is, from right to left), so that the needles form an X, with the right needle tip in front of the left needle tip.

2 Holding the crossed needles between your left thumb and forefinger, wrap the working yarn around the right needle from front to back and then to front again—in a counterclockwise direction.

3 Push the tip of the right needle to the back, carrying the new loop of yarn you just wrapped around it in step 2 through the cast-on stitch (a), and push the shaft of the right needle against the back of the shaft of the left needle to slide the cast-on stitch up and off the left needle tip (b). You now have 1 stitch on your right needle—your first purl stitch!

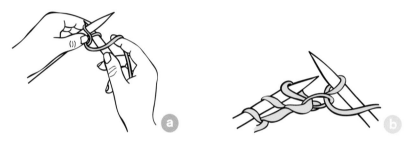

4 Repeat steps 1–3 for each remaining cast-on stitch, until all of the new purl stitches are on the right needle. When you have done that, you have purled 1 row.

btw: It may seem strange, but purling every row has the same effect as knitting every row: It creates garter stitch!

purl: continental style

Continental knitters say that purling is easier and quicker for them because wrapping the yarn takes just a flick of the finger. Combining knits and purls in the same row is definitely easier and quicker using this method—moving the yarn from front to back is a small, barely detectable motion—so do give this method a try.

Have your needles in position, with the yarn wound around your left hand, and then follow these steps:

1 Holding the working yarn in front of both needles, insert the right needle into the front of the first stitch on the left needle, from back to front (that is, from right to left), so that the needles form an X, with the right needle tip in front of the left needle tip.

2 Use your left forefinger to wrap the working yarn around the right needle from front to back, between the needles, and back to the front of the right needle.

note: This is a small motion, consisting of flicking your left forefinger down, bringing the yarn between the needles and then back up, and creating a loop on the right needle.

At first, it's hard to tell which stitches are knit stitches and which stitches are purl stitches. The easiest way to identify which is which is to recognize that knit stitches look like little Vs, and purl stitches look like bumps. So, if you're working in stockinette stitch (that is, knitting the right side rows and purling the wrong side rows), the smooth side made up of columns of Vs is the knit side; the bumpy side made up of ladders is the purl side. If you're mixing up knits and purls in one row to make ribbing, you knit the Vs and purl the bumps. If you're mixing up knits and purls in one row to make seed stitch, you purl the Vs and knit the bumps.

| Knit side | Purl side |

3 Push the tip of the right needle to the back, carrying the new loop of yarn you just wrapped around it in step 2 through the cast-on stitch (a), and push the shaft of the right needle against the back of the shaft of the left needle to slide the cast-on stitch up and off the left needle tip (b). You now have 1 stitch on your right needle—your first purl stitch!

4 Repeat steps 1–3 for each remaining cast-on stitch, until all of the new purl stitches are on the right needle. When you have done that, you have purled 1 row.

join new yarn

At some point, you're going to run out of yarn and need to start a new ball, or you're going to want to start using a new color to try your hand at stripes. But how do you do it? Don't worry—it's easy.

btw: You know it's time to change to a new ball if your first ball of yarn has length remaining that is less than four times the width of your knitting.

joining new yarn at the beginning of a row

It's a good idea to join a new yarn at the beginning of the row instead of in the middle. That way, you won't end up with a big center-stage knot puckering your knitting, and you'll have an easy time weaving in the loose ends. When you're ready to join new yarn, finish the row and cut the old yarn, leaving *at the very least* a 6-inch tail. You'll need that tail to weave in the end neatly and to protect your knitting from unraveling. Now you're ready to join the new yarn:

1. Tie a 6-inch end from your new ball snugly onto the tail of the old yarn.
2. Without confusing the new working yarn with the tied end, work across the row as usual. (At the finishing stage, you untie the knot and weave in the ends to tidy up. Page 21 describes how to weave in ends.)

joining new yarn in the middle of a row

There are times when you have no choice but to join a new yarn in the middle of a row. If you're knitting something circular, for example, you'll have to join midround. Just be sure to leave that 6-inch tail to weave in later. Assuming that you've gotten to the point where you've cut the old yarn and you're ready to start the new, here's how to join the new yarn midrow:

1. Work the next stitch using the new yarn, knitting it if it's a knit stitch or purling it if it's a purl stitch.
2. After you finish the row, tie the two 6-inch tails together somewhat loosely so that they don't unravel. (At the finishing stage, you untie the knot and weave in the ends, as described on page 21, to tidy up.)

bind off stitches

When you want to take your stitches off the needle permanently, without letting them unravel, you *bind off*. You can bind off at the very end of a project to finish it, or you can bind off a few stitches here and there to shape your knitting. Beginner knitters tend to bind off so tightly that the finished edge is completely inelastic and cinches in. It's good to bind off neatly but in a relaxed way that leaves your edge nice and flexible. You can bind off with knit stitches, which is called *knitwise*, or with purl stitches, which is called *purlwise*.

btw: If you're struggling with a too-tight bound-off edge, try using a larger needle for the bind-off row.

When you're ready to get those stitches off the needle nicely and neatly, don't forget to keep it loose; pulling up a little extra working yarn when you draw up a loop helps a lot. Here's how it works:

1. Knit until you have 2 stitches total on the right needle. Then insert the left needle tip from left to right into the front of the first stitch you knit.

Binding Off the Last Stitch

If you're binding off a whole row, as opposed to just a few stitches for shaping, you need to know how to bind off the last stitch. It's not hard: You bind off stitches until you have only 1 stitch remaining on the right needle and then cut the working yarn—leaving that 6-inch tail. You thread the tail through the last stitch and pull it tight. Voilà—you've bound off all of your stitches!

2 Use the left needle tip to pull that stitch up and over the second stitch and off the right needle (a). You should now have 1 stitch on the right needle (b), and you've bound off your first stitch knitwise!

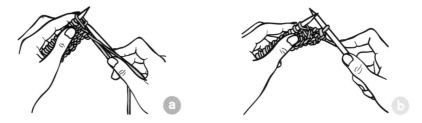

3 Repeat steps 1 and 2 until you have bound off the correct number of stitches.

Binding off purlwise is just like the knit bind–off, except you purl instead of knit. Some people find binding off purlwise a little looser than the knit bind–off.

weave in loose ends

By now you've probably completed a little piece of knitting of some sort. Those loose ends dangling from the sides look messy, right? You can tidy them up by weaving them in. Hopefully all of your ends are at least 6 inches long because you need that length to weave them in well.

You need a pair of scissors and a tapestry needle that is a suitable size for the thickness of your yarn. Sit down with these supplies and your knitted item and get weaving:

1 Thread the tail of yarn you're weaving in through the eye of the tapestry needle.
2 Weave the tapestry needle in and out of the backs of the stitches in a straight diagonal line for 2 to 3 inches.
3 Weave the tapestry needle in and out of the backs of the stitches in the opposite direction, next to the diagonal line from step 2.
4 Cut the yarn end close to the work, being careful not to snip your knitting.

knit with a double strand of yarn

Sometimes you'll want to knit with two strands of yarn at the same time. You can use two different yarns to create a unique yarn yourself, or you can use two strands of the same yarn to make it thicker and quicker to knit.

If you have only one ball of the yarn you want to knit double, you can pull ends from both the inside of the ball and the outside, and hold them together; or you can wind the yarn into two balls and hold together a strand from each ball. You do everything—casting on, knitting, and purling—as you would with a single yarn, only you hold both strands together as if they're one and knit and purl both strands at the same time.

show off with knit and purl

Now that you know how to knit and purl, why don't you impress your friends and learn some new stitch patterns? You can create a whole world of new patterns using just knits and purls. Some of the easiest knit/purl combinations result in complex-looking textures.

Here are a few basic stitch patterns for you to try. Trying them will really help you improve your knitting and purling skills—and your ability to identify knit and purl stitches. Start out with a pair of needles and a smooth, medium-color yarn that is suited, size-wise, to your needles. Make a little swatch of each stitch pattern by starting out with a number of stitches that equals about 4 inches. (For example, if your yarn ball says 18 stitches equals 4 inches, cast on 18 stitches.)

garter stitch

Garter stitch is the easiest stitch pattern, but that doesn't mean it's not a good one. It always lies perfectly flat, and it looks the same on both the front and the back, so it's reversible.

Watch your swatch grow as you knit. After several rows, horizontal ridges appear. Two knit rows make one ridge. Here's how it works:

> **Row 1 (right side):** Knit.
> Repeat row 1 for garter stitch.

stockinette stitch

Stockinette stitch is the pattern that most plain sweaters are made of. A smooth, flat surface made up of rows and rows of Vs forms the front—in knitting, this is called the *right side*. Rows of bumps make up the back, called the *wrong side*. Here's how you do it:

Row 1 (right side): Knit.
Row 2 (wrong side): Purl.
Repeat rows 1 and 2 for stockinette stitch.

btw: If you lose track of what row you're on, remember: Knit the Vs and purl the bumps.

reverse stockinette stitch

Reverse stockinette stitch is worked the same as regular stockinette stitch, only the bumpy side—the purl side—is considered the right side, and the smooth side is the wrong side. Here's what you do:

Row 1 (right side): Purl.
Row 2 (wrong side): Knit.
Repeat rows 1 and 2 for reverse stockinette stitch.

single rib

Single rib is the stitch pattern you see most often on cuffs, hems, and neckbands. Ribbing in general is very stretchy, so it works well in those areas. For this single rib, you need to cast on an even number of stitches (like 10, 12, 14, and so on). Here's how you do it:

Row 1 (right side): *Knit 1, purl 1; repeat from * to the end of the row.
Repeat row 1 for single rib on an even number of stitches.

double rib

Double rib has the same stretchiness as single rib, but the ribs are wider, so it's a bolder statement. For this double rib, you need to cast on a number of stitches that is divisible by 4 (like 12, 16, 20, and so on). Here's what you do:

Row 1 (right side): *Knit 2, purl 2; repeat from * to the end of the row.
Repeat row 1 for double rib over a number of stitches divisible by 4.

seed stitch

Seed stitch creates a fun bumpy fabric that lies flat and looks the same on both sides. It's worked almost like single rib, except instead of knitting the knits and purling the purls, you knit the purls and purl the knits to create a tiny checkerboard. For this version of seed stitch, you need an even number of stitches (like 10, 12, 14, and so on). Here's how you do it:

> **Row 1 (right side):** *Knit 1, purl 1; repeat from * to the end of the row.
>
> **Row 2 (wrong side):** *Purl 1, knit 1; repeat from * to the end of the row.
>
> Repeat rows 1 and 2 for seed stitch over an even number of stitches.

garter rib

Garter rib is a fun pattern that you don't see as often as you should. It's really easy, and it makes a nice stripy fabric. Even though it's called a rib, it doesn't pull in like ribbing. It lies flat and looks the same on both sides. You work it on a multiple of 4 stitches plus 2 (like 14, 18, 22, and so on). Here's what you do:

> **Row 1 (right side):** Knit 2, *purl 2, knit 2; repeat from * to the end of the row.
>
> Repeat row 1 for garter rib.

Binding Off in Pattern

Knitting instructions often say "Bind off in patt" (or "BO in patt"). That means you should continue working your stitch pattern at the same time that you bind off. Your finished project will have a sophisticated look, and ribbings and other knit and purl patterns will hold on to their stretch.

Say you're working in single rib—knit 1 stitch, purl 1 stitch. To bind off, you knit 1 stitch, then purl 1 stitch. Then you take the knit stitch up and over the purl stitch and off the right needle. Then you knit 1 stitch. Then you take the purl stitch up and over the knit stitch and off the right needle. And so on.

Chapter 3

oops! spotting and fixing mistakes

Everyone makes mistakes, even the experts. You're knitting away, chatting happily, and you unconsciously drop a stitch, twist a stitch, or even accidentally create extra stitches. If a mysterious hole suddenly appears in your knitting, you've probably yarn-overed by accident or dropped a stitch.

If one of these things happens, you have a couple of options: You can ask a knitter who knows how to correct errors to fix it or you can learn how to fix it yourself. The second option will carry you through nicely because you'll be able to fix your knitting no matter where you are. And once you see how simple it is to remedy these common mistakes, you won't have an anxiety attack next time it happens. Just open up the book to this page, and use this section as your very own knitting repair manual.

It's easiest to fix mistakes if you discover them early because you'll have less reworking to do. If you find an error further down, though, you can decide whether it bothers you enough to fix it. Some mistakes aren't that bad; you might be the only person who even notices something is amiss. Other mistakes, like those that will affect how the garment fits or that will make your knitting come undone, should be repaired.

too many stitches

This happens a lot with beginner knitters: You're knitting your first project, a scarf, and it starts out about 5 inches wide, with 20 stitches on the needle. After several inches, it's grown in width to about 8 inches, and there are 32 stitches on the needle. How did that happen?

It probably has to do with how you're holding the working yarn when you begin a new row. If you're pulling the working yarn *over* the top of the needle so that it's hanging down *behind* the needle, you're causing the first stitch to pull up onto the needle so that it looks like 2 stitches. When you begin a new row, make sure the working yarn is at the front of the needle, hanging down straight. When you pull it back to knit the first stitch, or to the front to purl the first stitch, bring it under the left needle, not over it. Check that the first stitch is really just 1 true stitch.

The first picture shows what it looks like when the working yarn is in the wrong place, and the second picture shows what it looks like when the working yarn is in the right place.

Wrong: Working yarn is draped over the needle and hanging down behind

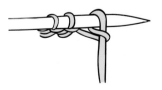

Right: Working yarn is in front of the needle, hanging straight down

btw: If you end up with too many stitches, you can do a couple of different things. You can look at the knitting as a learning swatch and proceed happily without reducing back to the original number of stitches. Or, if you have increased only a few stitches, you can knit 2 together the number of times necessary to get back to the original stitch count. (You'll learn all about the knit 2 together decrease on page 33.) Space the decreases evenly across the row or over several rows. Your knitting may look a little funky at that spot, but it may be better than unraveling all the way back to the beginning.

twisted stitches

When stitches get twisted, your knit fabric looks uneven. The first thing you need to know before you can even recognize the problem is how stitches should sit on the needle.

Hold your needle up horizontally and look at all the stitches sitting on it in a row. The right side of each loop should rest on the front of the needle, and the left side of each loop should rest against the back of the needle. The illustrations below show what twisted knit and purl stitches look like.

Twisted knit stitch   Twisted purl stitch

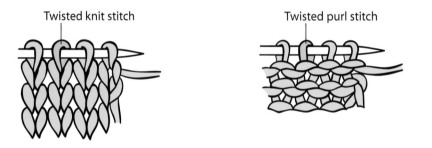

Another way you can tell you have a twisted stitch is if when you're knitting or purling, you get a little resistance from the stitch. It just doesn't feel right. As you become more experienced, you'll be able to see *and* feel a twisted stitch.

Follow these steps to fix a twisted stitch on the row after you twisted it:

1. Work across the stitches on the left needle until you get to the twisted stitch.
2. Using the right needle, pick up the twisted stitch from the left needle (a), turn it around, and place it back on the left needle so that the right side of the loop is in front (b).

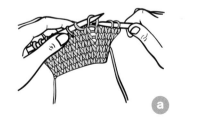
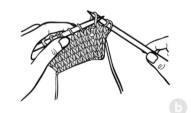

incomplete stitches

A stitch is incomplete when the working yarn doesn't get pulled through the loop. The stitch gets shifted from the left needle to the right needle but is not knit or purled, and the working yarn is wrapped over the needle, crossing over the incomplete, slipped stitch.

Here's how to repair an incomplete stitch on the row after you slipped it:

1 Work across the stitches from the left needle until you get to the incomplete stitch.

2 Insert the right needle as if to purl—from back to front—into the incomplete stitch.

3 Pull the incomplete stitch over the unworked strand and off the needle.

dropped stitches

A dropped stitch is a stitch that has slipped off your needles inadvertently. Everyone drops a stitch now and then—and this is a particular problem for beginner knitters—so don't feel bad if it happens to you.

Dropped stitches can unravel your knitting, so it's important to learn how to fix them. The easiest dropped stitch to fix is one that was dropped in the row below your current row because you can use your knitting needle to pick it up. If a stitch was dropped a few rows ago, causing a *run*, then you get to use a crochet hook to fix the problem. You should feel vastly pleased with yourself when you pick up your first dropped stitch on your own.

picking up a dropped stitch in the row below

If you drop a stitch and catch it when it's in the row below your current row, quickly insert a stitch holder or safety pin into the loop of the dropped stitch so that it doesn't unravel further.

Dropped stitch   Ladder

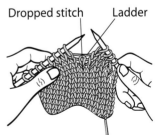

picking up a dropped knit stitch in the row below

If you're repairing a dropped knit stitch, pick it up as follows:

1 Work across the stitches on the left needle until you get to the dropped knit stitch.

2 Remove the stitch holder or safety pin and insert the right needle into the dropped stitch and under the horizontal strand (the "ladder") behind the dropped stitch.

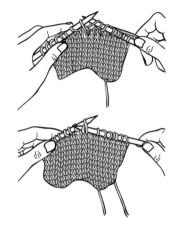

3 Insert the left needle from back to front into the dropped stitch on the right needle and pull it over the ladder and off the right needle.

4 Use the right needle to transfer the repaired stitch back to the left needle. You did it! The repaired knit stitch is ready to be worked as usual.

picking up a dropped purl stitch in the row below

Here's how you pick up a dropped purl stitch from the row below:

1 Work across the stitches on the left needle until you get to the dropped purl stitch.

2 Insert the right needle into the dropped stitch, as if to purl, and under the horizontal strand (the "ladder") in front of the dropped stitch.

3 Use the left needle to lift the dropped stitch on the right needle up over the ladder and off the right needle.

4 Insert the left needle into the back of the repaired stitch to transfer it back to the left needle. You did it! The repaired purl stitch is ready to be worked as usual.

picking up a dropped stitch several rows below

If you dropped a stitch several or more rows below, you have a run, which looks like a ladder. It's actually kind of fun to fix a run. To prevent the dropped stitch from running further, insert a stitch holder or safety pin into the loop of the dropped stitch. You need a crochet hook that is similar in size to your knitting needles to pick up the stitch and get rid of the run. Here's what you do:

1. Work across the stitches from the left needle until you get to where the dropped stitch should be.

2. Insert the crochet hook from front to back into the dropped stitch. Pull the lowest horizontal ladder from back to front through the dropped stitch.

3. Repeat step 2 until you have no more ladders left.

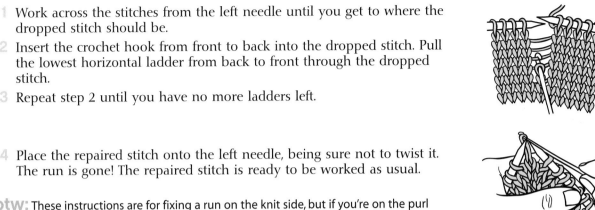

4. Place the repaired stitch onto the left needle, being sure not to twist it. The run is gone! The repaired stitch is ready to be worked as usual.

btw: These instructions are for fixing a run on the knit side, but if you're on the purl side when you discover a run, just flip your work to the knit side and follow the same steps to fix it.

how to unravel stitches

Some mistakes are too weird to be fixed using any of the previous methods. When you find a mistake that you are unwilling to live with, you can unravel your knitting back to where the mistake happened and rework from there.

unraveling stitch by stitch

When you find an error in the same row you're working on, you're lucky! You only have to unravel stitch by stitch back to the problem. When you get good at unraveling stitch by stitch, it will feel like you're knitting backward.

Here's how to unravel stitch by stitch on the knit side:

1. Hold the working yarn in back and insert the left needle from front to back into the stitch in the row below the next stitch on the right needle.

2. Drop the stitch above the right needle and pull the working yarn to un-knit it.

btw: To unravel stitch by stitch on the purl side, you do the same thing, only you hold the working yarn at the front of the work.

unraveling row by row

If you make a mistake that is more than 1 row down from your current row, unraveling stitch by stitch back to that point will take so long that you might want to give up on the project. Instead, you need to unravel row by row.

Many knitters simply slide the stitches off the needle, pull the working yarn to unravel back to the row before the error, and then reinsert a needle back into the stitches. You can do it that way, or, if releasing the stitches from the safety of the needle is too scary, you can do it by following these steps:

1 Take a circular needle that is thinner—two or three sizes smaller should work—than your working needles and weave it in and out of the stitches in the row below the point to which you would like to unravel.

btw: When weaving the needle under and over, take care to stay in the same row and to weave the needle under the right side of each stitch and over the left side of each stitch, or your stitches will get twisted.

2 Count your stitches to make sure you have picked them all up.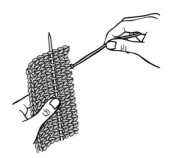
3 When the entire row is on the needle, pull the working yarn to unravel the rows above the needle. You have now unraveled back past your error, and you have an entire row of knitting on the needle.
4 Resume knitting with the working needles.

Chapter 4
knitting beyond the rectangle: increasing and decreasing

You know how to knit and purl, and you know how to combine knits and purls to make eye-catching stitch patterns, but where do you go from here? You probably want to learn how to make something other than a rectangle at this point. If that's the case, it's time to learn some shaping techniques, also known as increasing and decreasing.

There are lots of different ways to increase and decrease, each with its own purpose and result. This section includes a few basic increases and decreases—enough to get you through most shaping situations.

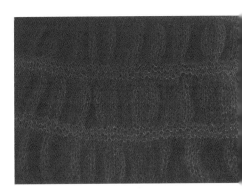

increasing

Increasing, or adding stitches, is what you do when you want to make your knitting wider. The majority of increasing occurs on the front side, on the edges, and it is easiest to keep track of increases when you do it that way. More complicated shaping, or shaping that involves increasing a whole bunch of stitches at once, takes place inside the edges.

btw: You can increase right on the edge, but if you make your increases 1 or 2 stitches in from the first stitch, your edges will look smoother and neater.

bar increase

This increase is called a *bar increase* because doing it creates a horizontal bar of yarn where the increase occurs. In some knitting instructions, it is called *kfb*, which stands for knitting into the front and back of a stitch. You should definitely knit 1 or 2 stitches at the beginning of the row before making a bar increase because it makes a kind of jagged edge if you don't. Here's how you work a bar increase:

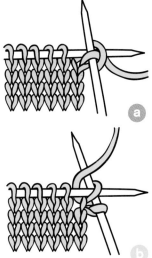

1   Insert the right needle into the next stitch and knit it, except don't bring the old stitch up and off the left needle (a); then insert the right needle into the back of the same stitch and knit it again ( ).

2   Bring the stitch you knit into twice off the left needle. You should now have 2 new stitches on the right needle, made from 1 stitch—the stitch you knit into the front of the stitch and the stitch you knit into the back of it.

make one

A make one increase (abbreviated m1 in knitting patterns) is less visible than a bar increase. You make it in between 2 stitches, so you have to do it at least 1 stitch in from the first stitch of the row. Here's how you make one:

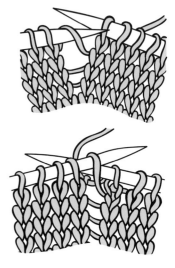

1 Use the left needle to pick up the horizontal strand, from front to back, between the last stitch worked on the right needle and the next stitch to be worked from the left needle.
2 Insert the right needle into the back of the loop and knit it.

yarn over

A yarn over (yo) is an increase that makes a hole, known in knitting as an *eyelet*. If you need to make your knitting wider but don't want a hole in it, don't use this one. Yarn over can also be used just for hole-making—in buttonholes and lace patterns, for example.

yarn over before a knit stitch

Here's how you make a yarn over before a knit stitch:

1 Bring the working yarn to the front of the needles and lay it over the right needle from front to back.
2 Knit the next stitch. (Laying the yarn over the right needle creates another stitch.)
3 On the next row, knit or purl the yarn over strand as usual.

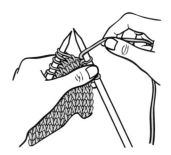

btw: The simple act of putting the yarn over the needle is the increase.

yarn over before a purl stitch

Here's how you make a yarn over before a purl stitch:

1 Bring the working yarn to the front of the needles, wrap it over and under the right needle, and bring it back to the front, ready to purl. (Looping the yarn around the right needle creates another stitch.)
2 Purl the next stitch.
3 On the next row, knit or purl the yarn over strand as usual.

decreasing

Decreasing is what you do to make your knitting narrower. Again, there are numerous ways to decrease, and there's not room in this book to cover all of those ways. The decreases that follow are good all–purpose decreases that you're likely to see in patterns.

Knit 2 together and purl 2 together are the most commonly used decreases. You can get by for a long time with just these two.

knit 2 together

A knit 2 together (abbreviated k2tog in knitting patterns) is used with—you guessed it—knit stitches, and it slants a little to the right on the front of your knitting. Here's how you do it:

1 Insert the right needle, as if to knit, into the front of the next 2 stitches on the left needle.
2 Wrap the yarn around the right needle and knit the 2 stitches as 1 stitch. You made 2 knit stitches into 1!

purl 2 together

The purl 2 together (abbreviated p2tog in knitting patterns) is for decreasing purl stitches, and it also slants a little to the right on the front of your knitting. Here's how you do it:

1 Insert the right needle from back to front (as if to purl) into the front of the next 2 stitches on the left needle.
2 Wrap the yarn around the right needle and purl the 2 stitches as 1 stitch. You made 2 purl stitches into 1!

Slip a Stitch

Some decreases and stitch patterns call for slipping a stitch. *Slipping* a stitch is simply moving a stitch from the left needle to the right needle without working it. Even though the stitch is not knit or purled, you can slip it knitwise or purlwise. To slip a stitch knit-wise, insert the right needle into the front of next stitch on the left needle, as if to knit, and just bring it off the left needle and onto the right. Likewise, to slip a stitch purlwise, simply insert the right needle from back to front, as if to purl, into the next stitch on the left needle. Bring the stitch up and off the left needle and onto the right. Now, the next time you see "sl 1," "slip 1 st knitwise," or "slip 1 st purlwise," you'll know what that means—and you'll be able to do it!

slip, slip, knit

Slip, slip, knit (abbreviated ssk in knitting patterns) is a fun little decrease that's almost invisible. It slants ever so slightly to the left, so it's a good counterpoint to a knit 2 together, if you have to shape something symmetrically, like a triangle or a pair of armholes. Here's how you do it:

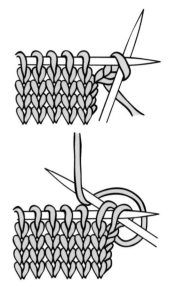

1 Insert the right needle from front to back into the front of the next stitch on the left needle and slip it onto the right needle.

2 Repeat step 1. You have just slipped 2 stitches, knitwise, to the right needle.

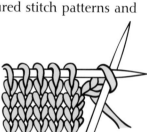

3 Now insert the left needle, from left to right, into the fronts of both slipped stitches and then knit them together as 1 stitch.

slip 1, knit 1, pass slipped stitch over

Slip 1, knit 1, pass slipped stitch over is another decrease that comes up pretty often. You see it in instructions for shaping certain armhole styles, and it's also often used in textured stitch patterns and lace. It is also referred to as slip, knit, pass. Here's how it works:

1 Insert the right needle from front to back into the front of the next stitch on the left needle and slip it onto the right needle.

2 Knit the next stitch from the left needle.

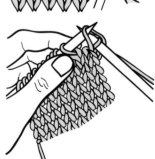

3 Insert the left needle into the front of the slipped stitch and bring the slipped stitch over the knit stitch and off the right needle.

btw: In knitting patterns, you'll see this decrease referred to as skp, and you'll see the abbreviation psso for pass slipped stitch over.

shaping with short-rowing

Short-rowing is a shaping technique that involves working a series of partial rows—instead of decreasing or increasing stitches—to create curved or slanted edges. Short–rowing is often used to shape sock heels.

short-rowing on the knit side

Here's how you work short rows on the knit side of stockinette stitch or garter stitch:

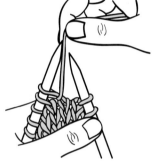

1. On the right side, work across the row to the point where the work should be turned. Keeping the working yarn at the back of the work, slip the next stitch from the left needle—as you would to purl—to the right needle.
2. Bring the working yarn between the needles to the front of the work.
3. Slip the same stitch you slipped in step 1 back to the left needle.
4. Bring the working yarn to the back of the work, thereby wrapping the slipped stitch.
5. Turn your work so that you're ready to work the wrong side.

short-rowing on the purl side

Here's how you work short rows on the purl side:

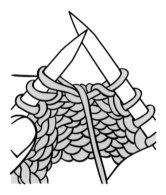

1. On the purl side, work across the row to the point where the work should be turned. Keeping the working yarn at the front of the work, slip the next stitch from the left needle—as you would to purl—to the right needle.
2. Bring the working yarn between the needles to the back of the work.
3. Slip the same stitch you slipped in step 1 back to the left needle.
4. Bring the working yarn to the front of the work, thereby wrapping the slipped stitch.

hiding the short-row wraps on the knit side

After you complete a short row, you need to hide your wraps so that your work looks tidy. This is often called "knitting the wraps together with the wrapped stitches." Here's how to do it on the knit side:

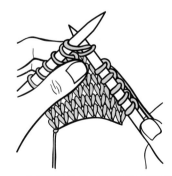

1. On the knit side, work to the point where the wrap is.
2. Insert the right needle knitwise under both the wrap and the wrapped stitch.
3. Knit the wrap and the wrapped stitch as 1 stitch.

hiding the short-row wraps on the purl side

Hiding your wraps on the purl side is often called "purling the wraps together with the wrapped stitches." Here's how you hide the short-row wraps on the purl side:

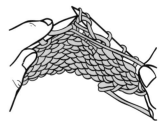

1 On the purl side, work to the point where the wrap is.
2 Insert the right needle from back to front through the back loop of the wrap. Lift the wrap and place it onto the left needle with the wrapped stitch.
3 Purl the wrap and the wrapped stitch as 1 stitch.

btw: After you complete your short-row shaping, you can bind off or continue your pattern as established.

Through Back of Loop

You will definitely come across the instruction to knit or purl a stitch or stitches "tbl," or "through back of loop." For a knit stitch or stitches, simply insert the needle from front to back into the back of the stitch or stitches. For a purl stitch or stitches, insert the needle from back to front into the back of the stitch or stitches.

stuff you should know
now that you can knit

By now you're knitting and purling away, casting on and binding off, weaving in ends, fixing mistakes, and even increasing and decreasing. But can you read knitting instructions and understand what they mean? Many beginners take one look at knitting instructions and give up immediately. All those abbreviations and unfamiliar terms look like another language. Plus, knitting authors are always going on and on about gauge, which involves *math*.

Come on, you want to be able to knit like the pros, right? Take a few minutes to look through the pages of this chapter to learn what all that stuff means. (You don't have to memorize it.) Then, when you move ahead to tackle a knitting project that involves (gasp!) following directions, you won't be completely in the dark.

all about gauge

If you're knitting a plain scarf or a little rectangular bag, you can probably get away with not knowing much about gauge. But when you're ready to knit a sweater, hat, or something else where size and fit are important, you need to understand gauge. *Gauge*, called *tension* in some places, is the number of stitches and rows per inch in knitting.

getting gauge

A lot of variables affect gauge: Different thicknesses of yarn knit to different gauges, the same yarn knits to different gauges on different sizes of needles, and different knitters knit the same yarn on the same needles at different gauges. In addition to all that, different stitch patterns knit to different gauges. Ribbing and cables cinch in; seed stitch and lace expand. That's why it's so important to check your gauge by knitting a little square, called a *gauge swatch*, before you start a project that needs to be a certain size to fit properly.

A knitting pattern tells you what the gauge should be for that particular project. It will read something like "Gauge: 20 stitches and 30 rows to 4 inches in stockinette stitch on US 7 (4.5 mm) needles." For you to knit that thing so that it comes out the same size as the one in the pattern, you must knit to that same gauge. If you are getting fewer stitches per inch than the pattern's gauge, your version will come out larger than it should. If you are getting more stitches per inch than the pattern's gauge, then your version will come out smaller.

Even a slight difference in gauge can have a big effect on the outcome. For example, say the gauge is supposed to be 5 stitches per inch, and you're supposed to cast on 100 stitches for a sweater back, so that it ends up 20 inches wide. If you're getting 6 stitches per inch—only 1 stitch per inch more—your version will turn out 16½ inches wide. That's a big difference! Even a difference of ½ stitch per inch can take a toll, so it's important to check and swatch until you get an accurate gauge before launching into a project where gauge is critical.

btw: Don't think that the gauge listed on the yarn label is the gauge you're going to get knitting that yarn on the recommended size needle. All knitters are different: It's more than likely you won't get that gauge your first try, and you'll have to swatch, swatch again.

If you're having a hard time understanding what a difference gauge can make, look at the swatches shown here. They were all knit using 20 stitches and 30 rows, but with different thicknesses of yarn on different sized needles. You can see how different their sizes are. That's why it's so important to make sure you have chosen yarn that will actually knit to the same gauge as the pattern and to check to be sure the gauge is correct. It would be a shame to spend weeks on a project, only to find that it doesn't fit because you didn't check the gauge first.

make and measure a gauge swatch

Please don't consider it optional to make and measure a gauge swatch before you begin a project. This small square of knitting that you'll use to measure how many stitches and rows per inch you are getting with your yarn and needles takes a short time to make, and it will save you a world of time and frustration later.

Some knitters save their swatches in a knitting diary or use them to test how the yarn washes or felts. You can even save up a whole bunch and sew them together into little blanket or pillow cover.

how to make a gauge swatch

To make a gauge swatch, start with the yarn and needle size the pattern calls for. It's actually a good idea to have ready three pairs of needles: the size called for, the next smallest size, and the next largest size.

Here's what you do:

1. Cast on the same number of stitches that the pattern says is equal to 4 inches.
2. Work in stockinette stitch (knit on the right side and purl on the wrong side) until the swatch is 4 inches long (measuring from the cast-on edge to the needle).
3. Bind off your stitches somewhat loosely, cut the working yarn (leaving about a 6-inch tail), and pull the tail through the last stitch.

What if Your Gauge Is Not What It Should Be?

If your swatch tells you that you are getting more stitches per 4 inches than your pattern calls for, try switching to a needle that is one size larger. If you are getting fewer stitches per 4 inches than the pattern calls for, try switching to a needle that is one size smaller. Make a new gauge swatch and remeasure.

how to measure a gauge swatch

Now that you have knit a gauge swatch, it's time to measure it. Before you measure, however, check to make sure it feels and looks good. If it's too stiff or loose for the project—even if the gauge is correct—you might want to try a different yarn. If the swatch meets your approval, move on to the following steps.

btw: It is difficult to match both stitch and row gauge, but it is more important to match the stitch gauge accurately. If your stitch gauge is correct but your row gauge is slightly off, just keep in mind that you should check your vertical measurements as you're knitting the project to stay on track.

Here's how you measure a gauge swatch:

1. Lay your swatch on a flat surface. Place a ruler or your stitch and needle gauge so that it's centered horizontally and vertically on the swatch.
2. Count how many stitches there are in a horizontal 2-inch space and how many rows there are in the vertical 2-inch space.
3. Divide these numbers by 2, and that is the number of stitches and rows you are getting *per inch*.
4. Multiply the per-inch number of stitches by 4 to check if you're getting what the pattern says should be the number of stitches equal to 4 inches.

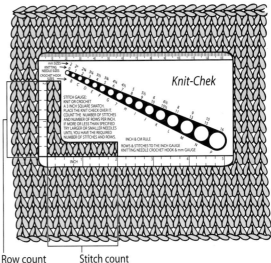

Row count   Stitch count

how to read knitting patterns

Knitting patterns are like recipes for cooking up certain knit designs. A knitting pattern contains all the information you need to make the knitted item: the sizes the design can be knit for, the materials and tools you need in order to make it, special techniques used in the design, and instructions that tell you how to do it.

So you can better find your way through your next knitting pattern, take a minute to get familiar with what you'll find in it.

skill level

Not all patterns list the skill level. If they do, they generally list categories such as the following:

Beginner: Good for first-time knitters. Includes little shaping and uses basic knit and purl stitches.

Easy: Still uses pretty basic stitches or easy stitch pattern repeats, easy color work (like stripes), and easy shaping and finishing.

Intermediate: May include a few different stitch patterns, or simple lace, cables, or intarsia. Might involve using double-pointed needles for circular knitting. Includes more advanced shaping and finishing than the previous level.

Experienced: Includes more complicated stitch patterns, sophisticated techniques, intricate color work (like Fair Isle), complex cables, lace or intarsia, and complicated or short-row shaping.

size/measurements

One of the first things listed in a pattern is the size or sizes at which it can be knit. This information is frequently represented by measurements: chest circumference for sweaters; length and width for scarves, blankets, bags, and shawls; and circumference for hats and skirts. Sometimes baby and kids' patterns list the age range for the sizes, along with the measurements.

Many knitting patterns are written for more than one size. In this case, the smallest size is listed first, with the remaining sizes listed in parentheses—for example, S (M, L). Throughout the pattern, the instructions contain information pertaining to the various sizes, such as stitch counts and numbers of decreases or increases, using the same format. For example, a pattern written for S (M, L) could instruct you to cast on 40 (50, 60) stitches. That means if you're knitting the medium size, you cast on 50 stitches.

btw: To avoid getting confused and following the directions for the wrong size, go over your pattern with a highlighter, marking only the numbers that pertain to the size you're knitting.

Choosing a size in a sweater pattern can be tricky. You definitely want to measure yourself before deciding which size to knit. Just like store–bought clothes, sizing for knitting patterns can be all over the map. So get out your handy measuring tape and take the body measurements that are listed in the pattern. For a normal fit, choose the size that is 2 or 3 inches larger in circumference than your chest measurement. For a loose fit, choose the size that is 4 or 5 inches larger around. For a tight fit, pick the one that is 1 or 2 inches *smaller* than your measurement.

Some patterns also include *schematics*, or diagrams of the finished knit pieces. They show the measurements for each piece before they're sewn together. Schematics are a helpful guide when you're knitting your pieces: You can measure your knitting as you go along and compare it to the schematic to be sure you're on track.

materials

After the sizing information, you usually find a list of materials. This section includes everything you need to make the project: yarn type and amounts and all the needles, tools, buttons, and any other items required.

gauge

Gauge is usually listed on a pattern after the materials. By now you understand the importance of gauge. If you come across a knitting pattern that doesn't list the gauge, throw it out! It is impossible to place too much emphasis on the importance of achieving the proper gauge before beginning a new project. Almost every knitting project from here on should start with knitting a gauge swatch—unless it's a scarf or a washcloth and you don't care how wide it comes out.

btw: Did you read the section on page 37 about gauge? If you skipped it, turn back now and check it out.

stitch patterns and special instructions

The last thing on a pattern before the actual instructions begin might be the stitch patterns used in the project. For example, if the project is worked in seed stitch, row by row instructions for how to work seed stitch would be listed. Any special instructions or notes, like "this sweater is worked in the round up to the armholes and then worked back and forth after that," would appear here, too.

abbreviations and terms

By now you have probably seen some knitting instructions and wondered what it all means—so many abbreviations and unfamiliar terms! The more you knit from patterns, the more familiar all of this stuff will become. Besides, if it weren't for abbreviations, knitting patterns would go on and on forever.

Use this guide to look up abbreviations and terms as you go along, and you'll do just fine.

Abbreviation	Meaning	Abbreviation	Meaning
alt	alternate	pu	pick up
approx	approximately	pwise	purlwise
beg	begin(s)/beginning	rem	remain(s)/remaining
bet	between	rep	repeat(s)/repeated/repeating
BO	bind off	rev St st	reverse stockinette stitch
CC	contrasting color	RH	right hand
ch	chain	rnd(s)	round(s)
cm	centimeter(s)	RS	right side
cn	cable needle	sc	single crochet
CO	cast on	sk	skip
cont	continue(s)/continuing	skp	slip, knit, pass slipped stitch over (decrease)
dec	decrease(s)/decreasing	sk2p	slip 1, knit 2 together, pass slipped stitch over the knit 2 together (decrease)
dpn(s)	double-pointed needle(s)	sl	slip
foll	follow(s)/following	sl 1, k1, psso	slip 1, knit 1, pass slipped stitch over (decrease)
g	gram(s)	sl1k or sl1 kwise	slip 1 knitwise
inc	increase(s)/increasing	sl1p or sl1 pwise	slip 1 purlwise
k or K	knit	sl st	slip stitch(es)
kfb	knit into the front and back (increase)	ssk	slip, slip, knit (decrease)
k2tog	knit 2 together (decrease)	sssk	slip, slip, slip, knit (decrease)
kwise	knitwise	st(s)	stitch(es)
LH	left hand	St st	stockinette stitch/stocking stitch
lp(s)	loop(s)	tbl	through back loop
m	meter(s)	tog	together
m1	make one (increase)	WS	wrong side
m1 p-st	make one purl stitch (increase)	wyib	with yarn in back
MC	main color	wyif	with yarn in front
meas	measure(s)	yd(s)	yard(s)
mm	millimeter(s)	yfwd	yarn forward
mult	multiple	yo	yarn over
oz	ounce(s)	*	repeat starting point
p or P	purl	**	same as *, but used to separate * instructions from the new instructions
pm	place marker	( )	alternate measurements and/or instructions
prev	previous	[ ]	instructions that are to be worked as a group the specified number of times
psso	pass slipped stitch over (decrease)		

A

as established	Work in a particular pattern, as previously set.
as foll	Work as the following instructions direct.
as if to knit	Knitwise; insert the needle into the stitch the same way you would if you were knitting it.
as if to purl	Purlwise; insert the needle into the stitch the same way you would if you were purling it.
at the same time	Work more than one set of instructions simultaneously.
axis stitch	The center stitch between two increases or decreases.

B

bind off in patt	Work stitch pattern while binding off.
bind off loosely	Bind off without pulling the working yarn too tight, so that the finished edge is elastic.
block	Lay knit pieces out flat and dampen or steam them to form them to the proper shape and measurements.

C

change to larger needles	Use the larger needles specified in the pattern, starting with the next row.
change to smaller needles	Use the smaller needles specified in the pattern, starting with the next row.
continue as established	Continue to work the same pattern.

E

ending with a RS row	Work a right side row as the last row.
ending with a WS row	Work a wrong side row as the last row.
every other row	Work as instructed on alternate rows only.

F

fasten off	At the end of a bind-off, pull the yarn through the last stitch and tighten.
from beg	From the cast-on edge; usually used to direct where to start measuring a knitted piece.

J

join round	When knitting in the round, work the first stitch of the round so that the last stitch and the first stitch join, forming a circle.

K

knitwise	As if to knit; insert the needle into the stitch the same way you would if you were knitting it.

L

lower edge	Cast-on edge.

M

marker	Something used to mark a point in a stitch pattern or to mark a point in your knitting, whether a plastic ring stitch marker, safety pin, or tied piece of yarn.
multiple	The number of stitches necessary to achieve one pattern repeat.

(cont'd.)

P

pick up and knit	A method of picking up stitches, as for a collar or button band, where the knitting needle is inserted into the work, yarn is wrapped around the needle as if to knit, and the new loop is pulled through.
place marker	Slip a stitch marker onto the knitting needle to indicate special instructions regarding the stitch following; or place some other sort of marker, such as a safety pin or strand of yarn, to indicated where buttons will be.
purlwise	As if to purl; insert the needle into the stitch the same way you would if you were purling it.

R

reverse shaping	Shaping that's opposite the shaping already described. For example, when working something like a cardigan, where the fronts are mirror images of each other, instructions for shaping are given for one front; you need to reverse those instructions for shaping the other front.
right side (RS)	The side of the knitting that will show.

S

selvage	An extra edge stitch (or stitches) that will be used to make a more tidy edge or make it easier to seam.
slip stitches to holder	Put stitches onto a stitch holder, usually to be worked later.

T

turning ridge	A row of stitches, usually purled on the right side of stockinette stitch, where a hem will be folded under.

W

weave in ends	When finishing a project, sew loose ends in and out of the backs of stitches or into seams to prevent them from unraveling.
with RS facing	Work with the right side facing you; usually used when instructions are telling you to pick up stitches for a button band or collar.
with WS facing	Work with the wrong side facing you.
work across	Continue to work as established across the row of stitches or across a group of stitches on a holder.
work buttonholes opposite markers	When working the fronts of a cardigan, place markers on the side where the buttons will be sewn and work buttonholes on the other front, opposite the markers.
work even	Work without increasing or decreasing.
work to end	Finish the row or round.
work sts as they appear	Knit the knit stitches and purl the purl stitches.
working needle	The needle that is being used to knit or purl stitches.
working yarn	The yarn that is being used to knit or purl stitches.
wrong side (WS)	The side of the knitting that will not show.

Chapter 6

getting fancy with your knitting

If you're ready to jazz up your knitting with some fancy techniques, this is the chapter for you. You'll learn how to make (very easy) lace, and in no time, you can whip up an airy little shawl or an openwork scarf. You'll also learn how to knit with multiple colors, so if you're sick of knitting in one color, you can add one, three, or even seven more colors. Perhaps adding some dimension through cables is what you're after; you'll learn that, too.

lacy stuff

Knitting lace involves putting a lot of holes in your work—on purpose. Remember the yarn over from Chapter 4? You use a lot of those yarn overs, also called *eyelets*, to create lace. You can combine eyelets with decreases like knit 2 togethers, repeated at particular intervals, to form a whole world of lace patterns.

Keeping track of lace patterns can be tricky: The stitches don't all look like Vs and bumps, and there are holes everywhere. Here's a good opportunity to use your handy row counter and those little plastic split-ring markers. You can mark stitch pattern intervals as you go along, if necessary. Lace is looser than the knitting you've grown accustomed to, and it's liable to slip off the needles. You can use bamboo or wood needles to slow the slippage, but be sure to choose needles that have a true point for easier manipulation.

Don't be scared off by lace. Lots of really easy patterns look much fancier and more complicated than they are. Here are a few to get you started.

From Swatch to Scarf

Practicing these lace patterns is a good opportunity to try your hand at openwork. Instead of making sample swatches, why don't you make your experiment into an airy scarf? How many stitches you cast on depends on your yarn's gauge and on how wide you want the scarf to be. For example, say that you want to make a scarf that is 6 inches wide, and your yarn knits to 5 stitches per inch; you would cast on 30 stitches. To account for using a larger needle, and for the way lace expands, you would probably subtract a few stitches and cast on 25 or 26 stitches. Just remember to cast on an even number, an odd number, or the correct multiple, as needed for the pattern.

easy lace

You work this super-easy lace on an odd number of stitches. Every row is the same, so you don't even have to use a row counter. Working the lace with needles a size or two larger than your yarn calls for gives the fabric a nice loose feel.

> **Row 1:** K1, *yo, k2tog; repeat from * to end of row.
>
> Repeat row 1 to desired length. Bind off knitwise.

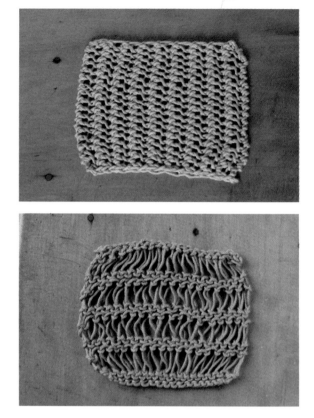

drop stitch pattern

This is a pattern you see on a lot of scarves. It also works well for belts, chokers, headbands, and bag handles. It's fun to work, and it grows in length very quickly. Plus, you can work it on any number of stitches. Try purling the wrong side rows for a different look.

> **Row 1 (RS):** Knit
>
> **Row 2 (WS):** Knit.
>
> **Row 3:** K1, *yo twice, k1; repeat from * to end.
>
> **Row 4:** Knit across, dropping the yo loops as you go.
>
> Repeat rows 1–4 to desired length. Bind off on a row 1 or 2.

color knitting

If you're bored using only one color in your knitting, it's time to talk about multicolor knitting. The easiest way to use more than one color in your knitting is to make horizontal stripes, changing colors every couple (or more) rows. That's fun, but if you're more ambitious, you can try *Fair Isle* knitting, which involves using two colors in the same row, or *intarsia*, which involves knitting motifs or pictures into your knitting.

Choosing colors that go well together can be hard for some people; for others, it's the most fun part of knitting. Just remember to choose colors that you or the person you're knitting for will actually want to wear; what's fun to knit and what's wearable can be two entirely different things, right? Hold the balls of yarn together to see how they look. Look in books, magazines, and catalogs to get color-combination guidance if you need it.

knitting horizontal stripes

Stripes are easiest to knit if each stripe is made up of an even number of rows. That way, color changes all occur along the same edge, so you can carry the yarn up the side of the work—saving you the bother of weaving in a zillion ends later. (Sometimes, having too many ends to weave in can mean *never* finishing a project!)

If you learned how to join new yarn a few chapters ago, then you can make stripes in your knitting. Here's how:

1 Work as many rows as you want the first stripe to be.
2 At the beginning of the next row, drop the working yarn and knit or purl across the row in the new color.

note: If your stripes are more than 2 rows each, carry the yarns up the side by twisting the first yarn around the second yarn at the edge of every other row. This way, the yarns will be at the ready when it's time to change colors again.

Knitting Stripes in Stitch Patterns

When you work stripes in ribbing or seed stitch, you get little bumps of the old color on all the purl stitches in the first row of the new color. If the little bumps bother you, you can avoid making them by knitting the first row of every color change instead of working it in the stitch pattern. You have to knit that first row on the right side for it to work, however. Here's how to do it: Using the desired stitch pattern, work as many rows as you want the first stripe to be, ending with a wrong side row. At the beginning of the next row, drop the old yarn and knit all stitches in the new color. Doing this has no adverse visible effect on the stitch pattern. Continue as established in the stitch pattern on the following row.

fair isle knitting

Fair Isle knitting, which probably originated long ago in Fair Isle, a remote and tiny island off northern Scotland, involves working with two colors across a row, carrying (or *stranding*) both of the yarns across the back. It takes a good deal of practice to master: If the yarns are pulled too tight across the back, the knitting can pucker and have no stretch; if the yarns are too loose, the stitches will look uneven, and you'll have a bunch of big loops hanging off the back that can get caught on things. That said, once you get the hang of Fair Isle, you can create beautifully patterned sweaters, hats, socks, and bags.

There are lots of different ways to knit Fair Isle. You can knit in your usual way, holding the yarn in one hand and alternating colors according to the pattern by dropping the color not in use. This is the easiest for a beginner, and you will get to see how the color pattern appears. However, this method can be slow going, and the yarns tend to get tangled up. Some knitters hold both yarns at the same time in one hand, with one color around the forefinger and the other around the second finger. This method, which requires a good deal of dexterity, is definitely worth a try. If you're really committed to learning Fair Isle, the best way is two-handed stranding, holding one yarn in each hand, working the English method and the Continental method at the same time to alternate colors without stopping. You end up with an impressively neat back, and it's easier to manage weaving in the color not in use.

With any of the Fair Isle methods, when you work more than 4 stitches successively in one color, or when you work in more than two colors per row, you may want to weave the color not in use in and out of the backs of every few stitches. This is simply a matter of positioning the non-working yarns so that the working yarn catches them up every 3 or 4 stitches.

If you take on too complicated a color pattern, or one that involves a lot of weaving in, Fair Isle might turn you off for good. So for now, let's just focus on learning Fair Isle using easier patterns that don't involve working more than 3 stitches in a row in the same color. To keep your color knitting from puckering, keep the stitches on the right needle spread apart so you can strand an adequate length of the non-working yarn across the back of them.

first things first: how to read a knitting chart

Most Fair Isle patterns appear as grid-like charts in knitting patterns. This can be confusing if you've never seen one before. For all stitch and color pattern charts, each square of a knitting chart represents a stitch, and a horizontal row of these squares represents a row of knitting. You read the chart the same way you work the knitting: from bottom to top and starting at the lower-right corner. The first horizontal row of squares represents a right side row—unless otherwise specified—and is read from *right to left*. The second horizontal row—a wrong side row—is read from *left to right*. For circular knitting, all chart rows are read from right to left. (Fair Isle is much easier in the round!)

Most charts represent only a small section of the knitting that is repeated to create the overall pattern. So, after you work the last stitch in a chart row, you return to the beginning of the same chart row and repeat. Working row–wise is the same: After you work the last row of the chart, you repeat the chart from the bottom.

A color pattern chart may contain an actual color in each square; more often, each color is represented by a symbol. A key to the symbols and colors accompanies the chart.

Key

☐ A

⦿ B

⊠ C

one-handed stranding on the knit side

Here's a quick lesson in how to strand the yarn when working Fair Isle holding the yarn with the same hand. Let's call the two different color yarns A and B, for clarity's sake. Here's how one–handed stranding works on the knit side:

1 Using yarn A, knit up to the point in the row where it's time to change colors. Drop yarn A, pick up yarn B and bring it above and over yarn A, and knit the correct number of stitches in yarn B.

2 When it's time to change back to yarn A, drop yarn B, pick up yarn A and bring it underneath yarn B, and knit until it's time to change color again.

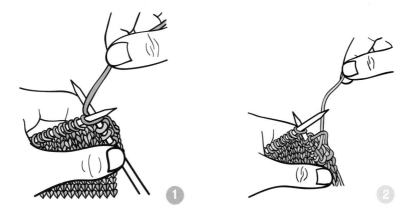

3 Repeat steps 1 and 2 across the row, always keeping yarn A underneath yarn B when changing colors, and being sure to carry both yarns to the end so that you can start the next row with either color.

one-handed stranding on the purl side

Here's how one-handed stranding works on the purl side:

1 Using yarn A, purl up to the point in the row where it's time to change colors. Drop yarn A, pick up yarn B and bring it above and over yarn A, and purl the correct number of stitches in yarn B.
2 When it's time to change back to yarn A, drop yarn B, pick up yarn A and bring it underneath yarn B, and purl until it's time to change color again.

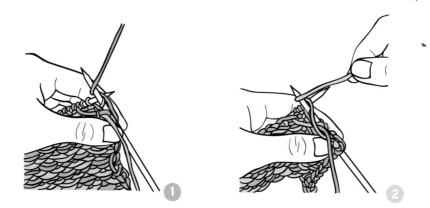

3 Repeat steps 1 and 2 across the row, always keeping yarn A underneath yarn B when changing colors, and being sure to carry both yarns to the end so that you can start the next row with either color.

two-handed stranding on the knit side

Do give two-handed stranding a try. It involves knitting and purling using both the English method and the Continental method at the same time, but it's so worth the effort. Plus, once you can knit both ways, you have a backup if your usual knitting hand gets sore!

Let's call the two different color yarns A and B, for clarity's sake. Here's what you do on the knit side:

1 Hold yarn A in your right hand, English style (see page 14), and yarn B in your left hand, Continental style (see page 15).
2 Knit with yarn A in your right hand, holding it above yarn B, to the point in the row where it's time to change colors.
3 Knit with your left hand using yarn B, which should automatically come from underneath yarn A.

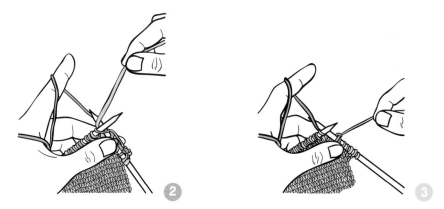

4 Repeat steps 1–3 across the row, being sure to carry both yarns to the end so that you can start the next row with either color.

two-handed stranding on the purl side

Here's how two-handed stranding works for the purl side:

1 Hold yarn A in your right hand, English style, and yarn B in your left hand, Continental style.
2 Purl with yarn A in your right hand, holding it above yarn B, to the point in the row where it's time to change colors.
3 Purl with your left hand using yarn B, which should automatically come from underneath yarn A.

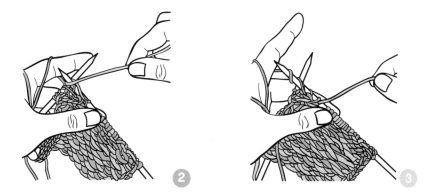

4 Repeat steps 1–3 across the row, being sure to carry both yarns to the end so that you can start the next row with either color.

intarsia knitting

Intarsia knitting, sometimes called *bobbin* knitting, is another form of color knitting. It's different from Fair Isle, where the colors are repeated and carried all the way across rows, in that the colors occur in isolated blocks, or as motifs against a solid or patterned background. You knit each motif using a separate ball or bobbin of yarn. Even if you're working a solid background, you need a couple of balls of background color: one for each side of the motif. It can be a little tricky to keep track of all the little bobbins of yarn hang–ing off your knitting, and you need to take great care to twist yarns together on the wrong side when changing colors to avoid ending up with holes where the colors meet.

Just as for Fair Isle, you work intarsia motifs from charts. You read the charts in the same direction as for all stitch pattern charts: from the bottom up and right to left for right side rows, left to right for wrong side rows. Unlike Fair Isle, however, intarsia is not easily worked in the round. (You end up with the motif yarn working yarn at the left side of the knitting, so when you get back around to the motif, you have to rejoin the yarn.)

Before you begin an intarsia project, wind your yarns onto two or three bobbins for each color. That way, you'll have enough to get going. Let's call the main color yarn A and the contrast color yarn B. Here's a quick set of steps to follow for a simple one–color motif:

1 On the right side, knit to the point in the row where the intarsia motif is to begin. Drop yarn A and get ready to knit with yarn B. If you need to temporarily tie yarn B to yarn A, that's okay.

2 Knit as many stitches in yarn B as your pattern calls for.

3 Drop yarn B and begin knitting from a new bobbin of yarn A. Work to the end of the right side row. Turn to the wrong side.

note: On subsequent right side rows, pick up the new color from underneath the old color to twist the yarns together on the back. This prevents a hole from forming.

4 On the wrong side, purl with yarn A to the point in the row where the color change should occur.

5 Drop yarn A, twist the yarns together by bringing yarn B up from underneath yarn A, and purl as many stitches in yarn B as the pattern requires.

6 Drop yarn B, twist the yarns together by picking up yarn A from underneath yarn B, and purl the next stitch. Continue as the pattern or chart instructs.

cable knitting

Cables in knitting are those things that look like braids of rope. Though they look difficult to do, you'll be surprised how easy it is to make a simple cable. If you can knit, purl, and slip stitches onto a holder, then you can make a cable! You work basic cables by holding stitches on a cable needle to the front or back of your work, knitting or purling the next stitches from the left needle, and then knitting or purling the stitches from the cable needle.

To practice making cables, you need smooth, medium–colored, medium–weight yarn, needles, a row counter, and a cable needle that suits your yarn size–wise.

basic six-stitch cable

This cable is called a back cross cable, or right cable, because the top of the cable "rope" crosses to the right. Start by slipping your row counter onto your knitting needle and casting on 10 stitches. You're going to have a 6–stitch cable in the center, with 2 stitches of reverse stockinette stitch on either side of it. Here's how you work it:

Row 1 (RS): Purl 2, knit 6, purl 2.

Row 2 (WS): Knit 2, purl 6, knit 2.

Row 3 (cable row): Purl 2, slip the next 3 stitches purlwise onto the cable needle and hold at the back of your work, knit the next 3 stitches from the left needle, use the right needle to knit the 3 stitches from the cable needle (starting with the first stitch that was slipped onto the needle), purl 2.

note: If knitting the stitches directly from the cable needle is too awkward, you can slip the stitches from the cable needle back onto the left needle before knitting them.

Row 4: Repeat row 2.

Repeat rows 1–4 for a back cross, or right, cable.

note: To make a front cross cable, also called a left cable, you work the same way except that you hold the stitches on the cable needle to the *front* of your work in row 3.

Now you can practice with some more easy cables, written in true knitting pattern style. Instructions for special cable maneuvers, accompanied by their abbreviations, appear at the beginning of each set of instructions.

medallion cable

For a medallion cable, start by slipping on your row counter and casting on 12 stitches. You're going to have an 8–stitch cable in the center, with 2 stitches of reverse stockinette stitch on either side of it.

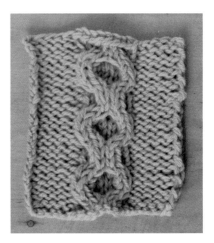

This cable uses the following abbreviations:

C4B (cable 4 back): Slip next 2 stitches onto cable needle and hold at back of work, knit next 2 stitches from left needle, then knit the 2 stitches from the cable needle.

C4F (cable 4 front): Slip next 2 stitches on cable needle and hold at front of work, knit next 2 stitches from left needle, then knit the 2 stitches from the cable needle.

Here's how you make a medallion cable:

> **Rows 1 and 5 (RS):** P2, k8, p2.
> **Rows 2, 4, 6, and 8 (WS):** K2, p8, k2.
> **Row 3 (cable row):** P2, C4B, C4F, p2.
> **Row 7 (cable row):** P2, C4F, C4B, p2.
> Rep rows 1–8 for medallion cable.

horn cable

To make a horn cable, start by slipping on your row counter and casting on 20 stitches. You're going to have a 16–stitch horn cable in the center, with 2 stitches of reverse stockinette stitch on either side of it.

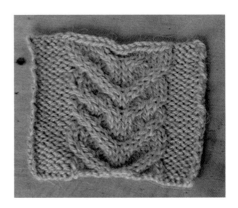

This cable uses the following abbreviations:

C4B (cable 4 back): Slip next 2 stitches onto cable needle and hold at back of work, knit next 2 stitches from left needle, then knit the 2 stitches from the cable needle.

C4F (cable 4 front): Slip next 2 stitches on cable needle and hold at front of work, knit next 2 stitches from left needle, then knit the 2 stitches from the cable needle.

Here's how you make a horn cable:

> **Row 1 (RS):** P2, k4, C4B, C4F, k4, p2.
> **Rows 2, 4, and 6 (WS):** K2, p16, k2.
> **Row 3:** P2, k2, C4B, k4, C4F, k2, p2.
> **Row 5:** P2, C4B, k8, C4F, p2.
> Rep rows 1–6 for horn cable.

bobble cable

Bobbles accent this fun cable. (See "Making a Bobble," below, to learn how to do it.) Start by slipping on your row counter and casting on 13 stitches. You're going to have a 9-stitch bobble cable in the center, with 2 stitches of reverse stockinette stitch on either side of it.

This cable uses the following abbreviations:

mb (make bobble): See "Making a Bobble," below, for instructions.

T3B (twist 3 back): Slip next stitch onto cable needle and hold at back of work, knit next 2 stitches from left needle, then purl the stitch from the cable needle.

T3F (twist 3 front): Slip next 2 stitches onto cable needle and hold at front of work, purl next stitch from left needle, then knit the 2 stitches from the cable needle.

T5BP (twist 5 back purl): Slip next 3 stitches onto cable needle and hold at back of work, knit next 2 stitches from left needle, then purl 1, knit 2 from the cable needle.

Here's how you make a bobble cable:

Row 1 (RS—cable row): P3, T3B, p1, T3F, p3.
Rows 2 and 8 (WS): K3, p2, k3, p2, k3.
Row 3 (cable row): P2, T3B, p3, T3F, p2.
Rows 4 and 6: K2, p2, k5, p2, k2.
Row 5 (bobble row): P2, k2, p2, mb, p2, k2, p2.
Row 7 (cable row): P2, T3F, p3, T3B, p2.
Row 9 (cable row): P3, T3F, p1, T3B, p3.
Rows 10 and 12: K4, p5, k4.
Row 11 (cable row): P4, T5BP, p4.
Rep rows 1–12 for bobble cable.

Making a Bobble

There are many ways to make bobbles, but this is the easiest. Work to the point where you want the bobble. Knit into the front, back, front, back, and front (that's five times) of the next stitch. Without turning your work, use the left needle to lift the fourth stitch and pass it over the fifth and off the right needle; pass the third stitch over the fifth and off the right needle; pass the second stitch over the fifth and off the needle; and finally, pass the first stitch over the fifth and off the right needle. Now you have a bobble on the right needle, and you're back to the original number of stitches.

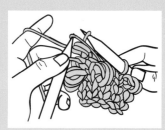

Chapter 7
knitting in circles

Have you ever seen someone knitting a sock or something else on 4 or 5 needles at once, with lots of points sticking out all over the place? You probably thought, "I could never do that." Well that was then, this is now. You know how to knit, purl, fix mistakes, knit with multiple colors, and a whole bunch of other knitting techniques that are much more difficult than *knitting in the round*—which is what you call knitting on all those needles at the same time.

You knit in the round, or circularly, when you want to knit a tube. Socks, mittens, and gloves are all tubes. Hats are also tubes, as are skirts. Sweater bodies can be tubes, too. What's great about knitting in the round is that you don't have to sew as many seams. Sometimes, the thing you knit is pretty much finished—except for maybe weaving in a few ends—as soon as you bind off or cut your yarn and pull it through the last stitches. That's a real bonus if sewing seams and weaving lots of ends is what keeps you from finishing a knitting project. Another nice thing about knitting in the round is that you're always working, around and around, on the right side. So, if you're making something in stockinette stitch, that means no purling!

You can knit in the round on circular needles or double-pointed needles. Sometimes, the same project will call for a circular needle *and* double-pointed needles, so it's good to learn how to work on both.

knit in the round on circular needles

Circular needles are long nylon or plastic cords with a needle tip on each end. You can get them in plastic, wood, bamboo, and metal—just like straight needles. The circumference of the project you're going to knit determines the length of needle you use. Usually, your pattern will tell you what length you need. For example, if you're going to make a skirt that is 32 inches in circumference, you'll probably want a 24- or 29-inch circular needle. You can't use a needle longer than your item's circumference, or your knitting will be all stretched out and frustrating to knit.

casting on with circular needles

Casting on with circular needles is very similar to casting on with straight needles, but it does require a little extra care. Here's what you do:

1 Cast on stitches to one end of the circular needle, using the same method you usually use.

2 When you have cast on the number of stitches you need, make sure the stitches are not twisted. Having the cast-on edge going around the inside of the needle when you hold the tips together is a good way to ensure this.

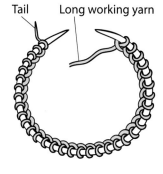

Tail   Long working yarn

btw: If the cord on your circular needle is curled up tightly, it will be a pain to work with. Put the cord under hot water for a minute, and then straighten it out.

knitting with circular needles

Now comes the fun part. Remember, to knit on circular needles, you knit in *rounds*, not rows. You actually knit a spiral, around and around.

btw: If your stitches are twisted around the circular needle and you start knitting away, you'll end up with the whole tube of knitting twisted, like a Mobius strip. This could be kind of a cool thing, but it might not be something you can actually wear. If that's not what you want, you'll have to start over at the cast-on row; it's not something you can fix in the middle of the project.

Follow these steps to join the round and knit with circular needles:

1 Hold the end of the needle that the working yarn is attached to in your right hand. Place a stitch marker after the last stitch that was cast on to show the end of the round.

note: A stitch marker can be either a plastic ring marker or a knotted piece of scrap yarn.

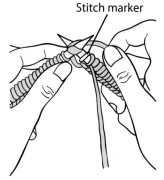

Stitch marker

2 Use the needle in your right hand to knit the first cast-on stitch from the needle in your left hand, giving the yarn a firm tug (on this first stitch only) so that the join is secure. Knitting this first stitch joins the round.

3 Knit all the way around until you reach the stitch marker. To begin the second round, slip the marker from the left needle to the right needle and keep knitting.

That's it! You just keep going, slipping that marker every round.

btw: If you lose the marker, a good way to find the end of the round is to look for the yarn tail left from casting on and run your finger up the stitches from there.

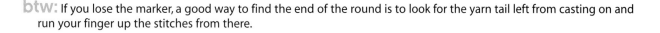

knit in the round on double-pointed needles

Circular needles have not been around since the beginning of time. Long ago, all circular knitting was done on double-pointed needles. These needles have no knob—just a point on each end—and come in sets of four or five. Like other knitting needles, they are made of plastic, metal, wood, and bamboo. Wood and bamboo are good for beginners because the needles don't slide out of your stitches easily when not in use. Metal double-pointed needles are not a good idea for a beginner knitter. Due to these needles' weight and slippery surface, they often slip out of the stitches, causing panic as stitches fall off the needle, ready to unravel.

Double-pointed needles are used these days mostly for small things like socks, mittens, and hats. For some tubular items, like certain hats, you start out on a circular needle and then switch to double-pointed needles when, after decreasing to shape the top, there are too few stitches for the circular. Here we look at how to use a set of four double-pointed needles; using a set of five is exactly the same except that you have four needles holding the knitting instead of three.

casting on with double-pointed needles

Casting on with double-pointed needles is similar to casting on with circular needles, except you divide the cast-on stitches over three double-pointed needles. The fourth, empty, needle is the working needle. Here's what you do:

1 Cast on the number of stitches you need onto one of the double-pointed needles. Then slip one-third (be approximate if your total number doesn't divide by three equally) of the stitches onto a second double-pointed needle and the remaining one-third to a third double-pointed needle.

note: If all the stitches you're casting on don't fit on one double-pointed needle, start slipping the first one-third to the second double-pointed needle when you run out of room.

2 Arrange the three needles in a triangle, with the needle with the working yarn attached on the right, the center needle at the base of the triangle, and the needle with the first cast-on stitch on the left. Make sure the stitches are not twisted.

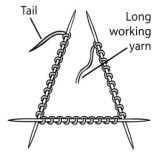

note: As with knitting on a circular needle, having the cast-on edge going around the inside of the triangle when you hold the tips together is a good way to ensure that the stitches are not twisted.

knitting with double-pointed needles

Knitting with double-pointed needles can feel unwieldy at first. Just stick with it through the awkward phase—it won't last long. Socks, mittens, and hats work up quickly and seamlessly with double-pointed needles, so it's really worth giving double-pointed needles a chance. Here's how it works:

1 Hold the triangle of needles with the needle with the working yarn attached to it on the right. Attach a split–ring marker or safety pin to the last stitch that was cast on to show the end of the round, if desired. Hold the needle with the first cast–on stitch on it in your left hand.

2 Using the fourth, empty needle, join the round by knitting the first cast–on stitch from the left needle, giving the working yarn a solid tug (on this first stitch only) so that the join is secure. Knitting this first stitch joins the round.

3 Knit all the way around, tugging slightly on the first stitch of each needle, until you reach the stitch marker. To begin the second round, attach the marker to the last stitch of the round and continue knitting.

Keep going, reattaching the marker every round.

btw: As with knitting on a circular needle, if you lose the marker, you can find the end of the round by looking for the yarn tail left from casting on and running your finger up the stitches from there. When you're working on double-pointed needles, the end of the round is almost always at the end of a needle.

make a knitted cord

Making a knitted cord, called an I–cord, is another kind of circular knitting, on a very tiny scale. You need only two double-pointed needles to do it, and the result is a tubular cord. You can use knitted cords for all kinds of things: button loops, bag handles, bows, and topknots on hats, to name just a few. Here's how you make one:

1 Cast on 5 or 6 stitches to a double-pointed needle.

2 Knit across the stitches with the second double-pointed needle. Do not turn the work to the wrong side.

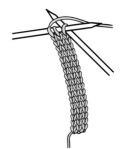

3 Push the stitches back to the other end of the double-pointed needle, so you're ready to work a right side row again. Insert the second double-pointed needle into the first stitch to knit as usual, and firmly pull the working yarn from the other end of the row, at the back, and knit the stitch. Knitting this stitch with the yarn pulled from the opposite end closes the tube.

4 Knit to the end of the row (well, round, actually!).

5 Repeat steps 3–4 until the cord is as long as you want it to be. You can end it by binding off or cutting the yarn (leaving a 6–inch tail) and pulling it through all the stitches and cinching together.

finishing touches

A lot of knitters say they hate finishing. *Finishing* is what you do when you're done with the knitting part of a project: It involves weaving in ends, which you learned about on page 21; blocking your knitted pieces so that they're straight, smooth, and neat; sewing the pieces together; and adding borders, buttonholes, and pockets. Try not to hate finishing. If you dive in with a positive attitude and get really good at it, you'll have a deeper sense of accomplishment and pride in your projects, and your knitting will be more wearable. You have spent many hours knitting that thing; you should spend a couple more on finishing to show off all that work in the best light possible.

block your socks off

Blocking, which involves getting your knitted pieces wet and then shaping and smoothing them to the correct measurements, works wonders. Blocking evens out uneven stitches, uncurls edges, and molds pieces to the correct measurements. It lets you open up and show off your lace and cable patterns, too. Don't skip the blocking phase, or you'll really be missing out.

Some knitters save all the blocking until the end—after seaming and picking up button bands and collars. The problem with this is that it's not as easy to block to measurements if you're dealing with double-thicknesses of sleeves and fronts and backs. It's really better to block before sewing seams: Seaming is easier and neater, and your knitted pieces get the attention they deserve. Later, a quick steam with an iron after all the finishing is done (minus sewing on buttons) smoothes out the seams and button bands, and it takes only a few minutes. The blocking techniques shown here are pretty painless, too. Neither method requires soaking your big project in a tub of water and then slogging it across the house to roll it in numerous towels. Here's what you need: your knitted pieces, an ironing board, a steam iron, a spray bottle, a light cloth (such as a pillowcase), your tape measure, and some rustproof pins—that's it!

steam blocking

Steam blocking is great because it's fast, and you don't have to wait a long time for your pieces to dry. Check your yarn's ball band to be sure that steaming your yarn is safe. (Remember that page 7 shows the ball band symbols for yarn care.) Steam blocking is good for wool, cotton, cashmere, and alpaca. You use the iron for steam—not for pressing. Just run it lightly above the knitting, barely touching.

btw: If you have an old iron that may emit dirty or rusty spray, steam the back of your knitting, laying a light cloth over it first. (Better yet, see if you can borrow a better iron!)

Here's what you do:

1 Lay a knitted piece flat on a padded surface. Pin at just enough points to hold the piece straight for now.

2 Measure the knitted piece to make sure it's the same size as the pattern says it should be. Adjust the pins, if needed, to even out the piece and match the measurements.

note: Don't stretch and pin ribbed cuffs and hems unless the pattern says to do so. If you stretch and block your ribbings, they will lose all their stretch.

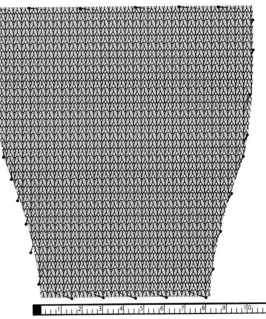

3 When the measurements are correct, pin the piece all around.

4 Cover the knitted piece with a light cloth. (You can dampen the cloth with a spray bottle if you want.) Slowly and gently, run the iron over the whole piece, avoiding the ribbing, and being careful not to press hard or distort anything.

5 Allow the piece to cool and dry and then remove the pins.

6 Repeat steps 1–5 for all the remaining pieces. Be sure everything is completely dry before sewing the seams.

easy wet blocking

Instead of blocking with an iron, you can wet block using this easy spray bottle method. You can do it on an ironing board, a counter top, or the floor—wherever you have the room. Again, make sure your yarn allows washing in water. This is a good method for most wools, blends, and hairy yarns like mohair or angora. Also, this method works better than steam for a highly textured or cable pattern.

You just do the following:

1 Lay a knitted piece flat on a padded surface. Pin at just enough points to hold the piece straight for now.

2 Measure the knitted piece to make sure it's the same size as the pattern says it should be. Adjust the pins, if needed, to even out the piece and match the measurements.

note: Again, don't stretch and pin ribbed cuffs and hems unless the pattern says to do so. If you stretch and block your ribbings, they will lose all their stretch.

3 When the measurements are correct, pin the piece all around.
4 Wet the piece thoroughly with a spray bottle.
5 Let the piece dry thoroughly and then remove the pins.
6 Repeat steps 1–5 for all the remaining pieces. Be sure everything is completely dry before sewing the seams.

it's sew easy: join knit pieces

There are lots of different ways to sew seams, and some seam techniques are better than others for different parts of your knitting or for certain stitch patterns. For example, if you're joining horizontal edges, like shoulders, you might want to use a different seam than you would use when joining vertical edges, like sweater side seams.

To sew your knitting together using any of these techniques, you use a tapestry needle and yarn (usually the same yarn used to knit your pieces). Tapestry needles come in a few sizes for different thicknesses of yarn. The point of the needle is rounded and blunt, unlike a sewing needle; that's so that you don't split your yarn and stitches when sewing. If you knit your project in a hairy novelty yarn or a very bulky yarn, you should find a plain, smooth yarn that matches it to sew seams. You'll go out of your mind trying to sew seams with hairy or bumpy novelty yarn.

Here are a few excellent seam techniques that should carry you through most situations and give your finished projects a sophisticated look.

btw: To be on the safe side, start with a length of yarn that is approximately double the length of your seam.

invisible horizontal weaving

Invisible horizontal weaving is good for joining one horizontal edge to another, like bound-off shoulder edges. You weave the needle in and out, imitating the knit stitches, so it is practically invisible. Here's how you make this seam:

1 Thread a tapestry needle with a long enough piece of yarn to sew the seam and leave about 6 inches coming out the eye.

btw: When you thread the tapestry needle to sew a seam, don't tie a knot in the end of the yarn. Instead, you'll weave in the ends when you're done (see page 21).

2 Lay your pieces on a table with the right sides up, lining up the bound-off edges horizontally. Insert the needle from back to front through the middle of the first stitch of the lower piece, pulling through until about 6 inches of yarn remain.

3 Use the needle to pick up the two loops (the V) of the corresponding stitch on the upper piece. Pull the yarn through, but not too tightly.

4 Bring the needle across the seam to the next stitch on the lower piece and use it to pick up the loops (the upside-down V), threading it through all the way.

5 Repeat steps 3 and 4 across the seam, pulling the yarn lightly—not too tightly, or it will pucker—every couple stitches to neaten it.

6 Weave in the loose ends.

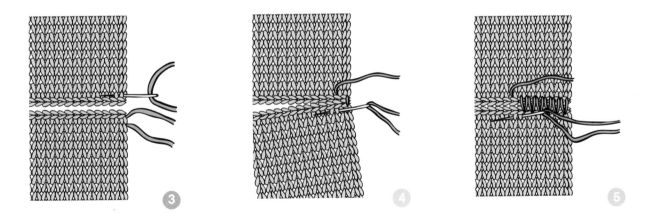

mattress stitch for stockinette stitch

Mattress stitch creates flat, invisible vertical seams, for things like sweater sides, sleeves, and hat seams. You use it to join the vertical edges of stockinette stitch. Here's how you make this seam:

1 Thread a tapestry needle with a long enough strand of yarn to sew your seam and leave about 6 inches of yarn coming out the eye.

2 Lay your pieces on a table with the right sides up, lining up the vertical edges to be joined. Sew 1 stitch at the base of the seam to join the pieces: Insert the needle from back to front through the space between the first and second stitches on the lower-left corner of the right piece, pulling yarn through until about 6 inches of yarn remain; insert the needle from front to back between the first and second stitches in the lower-right corner of the left piece; bring the needle back through the same spot on the right piece again. Pull the yarn through snugly.

3 Find the horizontal bar of yarn between the first and second stitches. Insert the needle under that horizontal bar, and the one above it, between the first and second stitches, on the right piece. Pull the yarn through.

4 Insert the needle under the corresponding horizontal bars on the left piece. Pull the yarn through.

5 Insert the needle under the next horizontal bar up on the right side and then under the corresponding bar on the left side. Continue in this manner, alternating from side to side, and pulling the yarn snugly every inch or so to tighten it, to the end of the seam.

6 Weave in the loose ends.

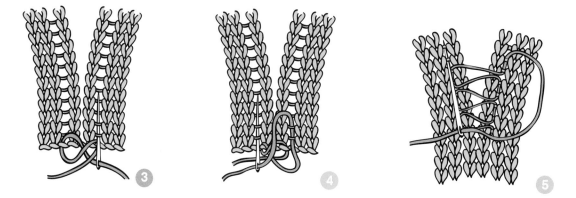

mattress stitch for garter stitch and reverse stockinette stitch

Joining vertical garter stitch and vertical reverse stockinette stitch edges is a little different than joining stockinette stitch seams. Instead of inserting the needle under the bar between stitches, you insert it right into the stitches.

See how the stitches look like smiles and frowns? To join these pieces, you insert the needle into the smile of one stitch and then into the frown of the corresponding stitch on the other side of the seam. Here's how it works:

1 Thread a tapestry needle with a long enough strand of yarn to sew your seam and leave about 6 inches of yarn coming out the eye.

2 Lay your pieces on a table with the right sides up, lining up the vertical edges to be joined. Sew 1 stitch at the base of the seam to join the pieces: Insert the needle from back to front through the space between the first and second stitches on the lower-left corner of the right piece, pulling yarn through until about 6 inches of yarn remain; insert the needle from front to back between the first and second stitches in the lower-right corner of the left piece; bring the needle back through the same spot on the right piece again. Pull the yarn through snugly.

3 Insert the tapestry needle up into the smile (the bottom loop) of the first stitch on the right piece and pull yarn through, but not too tightly.

4 Insert the tapestry needle up into the frown (the top loop) of the corresponding stitch on the left piece and pull the yarn through.

5 Repeat steps 3 and 4, pulling yarn snugly every few stitches to tighten it, until the seam is sewn.

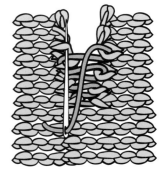

invisible vertical-to-horizontal weaving

You use this seam for sewing sleeve caps to armholes or when you need to sew a bound-off or cast-on edge to a vertical side edge. It's actually a combination of invisible horizontal weaving and mattress stitch because you join bound-off stitches to rows. Try it out:

1 Thread a tapestry needle with enough yarn to sew the seam. Place your pieces on a table, right sides up, and match the edges to be joined evenly. If you're sewing a sleeve cap to an armhole, line up the shoulder seam to the center of the sleeve cap. Pin together to hold them in place.

2 Working from right to left, and starting just inside the bound-off edge, insert the needle from back to front through the V of the first stitch of the lower piece and pull the yarn through until about 6 inches of yarn remain.

3 Now insert the needle under the corresponding bar between the first and second stitches of the upper piece and pull the yarn through, but not too tightly.

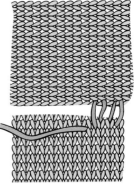

4 Bring the yarn across the join and pick up the loops that make the point of the upside-down V of the next stitch on the lower piece, pulling the yarn through, trying to imitate the size of each stitch below the bound-off edge.

5 Continue alternating back and forth between the upper and lower pieces until you finish the seam.

6 Weave in the loose ends.

note: Because you are matching rows to stitches in this join, and because there are usually more rows per inch than stitches, you need to pick up two of the bars on the horizontal piece every other stitch or so to keep the seam even.

backstitch

Backstitch is a good catchall seam. You can use it to join both horizontal and vertical edges. However, backstitching is similar to sewing fabric seams in that the pieces being sewn together overlap, so the seam is pretty bulky. If not done well, it can look uneven and messy. It's still a good technique to know, and if the other seam techniques are a little daunting for now, you can always rely on back-stitching to get your pieces firmly together. Here's how you do it:

1 Thread a tapestry needle with a long enough strand of yarn to sew your seam and leave about 6 inches of yarn coming out the eye.

2 Place the knitted pieces together, with the right sides facing each other and the seam edge lined up. Secure the edge stitches by bring the needle through both thicknesses from back to front, 1 stitch in from the edge. Do this twice and pull the yarn through.

3 Insert the needle through both thicknesses, from back to front, about 2 stitches to the left, and bring the yarn through.

4 Insert the needle from front to back, about 1 stitch to the right (that's why it's called *back*stitch), and pull the yarn through.

5 Bring the needle ahead 2 stitches to the left and insert it from back to front. Repeat steps 3 and 4 across the seam until you reach the end, taking care to insert the needle at the same depth every time.

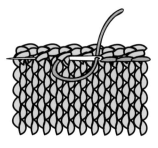

btw: Backstitch is kind of like making the needle take 2 steps forward (to the left) and then 1 step back (to the right) over and over again.

6 Weave in the loose ends.

btw: You can reduce the bulkiness of a backstitched seam somewhat by sewing with a matching-color yarn that is thinner than the yarn used to knit the pieces.

grafting

If you want to get really fancy, you can *graft* things like unshaped shoulders, sock toes, and mitten tips together, instead of sewing them. Grafting involves joining one open row of live stitches to another, while the stitches are still on the needles. You need to have the same number of stitches on each piece, and the final result looks just like a row of stockinette stitch, so it's invisible on the right side.

You can graft using Kitchener stitch or three-needle bind-off. Both can feel difficult to maneuver at first, but if you follow the instructions here step by step, you'll do fine—and you'll definitely feel pretty special.

kitchener stitch

Kitchener stitch seems very complicated at first, but once you get going, you realize there's a pattern to it, and it becomes easy. And it's worth the effort: You end up with a completely invisible join, with no bumpy seam. To join edges using Kitchener stitch, follow these steps:

1 Lay both pieces of knitting on a table, with the wrong sides down and the needles running parallel to each other, with the tips pointing to the right.

2 Using the same yarn you used to knit your pieces, thread a tapestry needle with a strand that is about twice the length of the seam.

3 Insert the tapestry needle into the first stitch on the lower needle as if to purl; pull the yarn through until about 6 inches remain. Leave the stitch on the needle.

4 Insert the tapestry needle into the first stitch on the upper needle as if to knit and pull the yarn through, leaving the stitch on the needle.

5 Insert the tapestry needle into the same first stitch on the lower needle again, this time as if to knit; then slip this stitch off the lower needle.

6 Insert the tapestry needle into the next stitch on the lower needle as if to purl, pulling yarn through and leaving the stitch on the needle.

7 Insert the tapestry needle into the first stitch on the upper needle again, this time as if to purl; pull yarn through and slip this stitch off the upper needle.

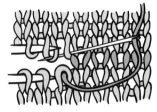

8 Insert the tapestry needle into the next stitch on the upper needle as if to knit, pulling yarn through, and leaving this stitch on the needle.

9 Repeat steps 5–8 until all the stitches have been grafted.

10 Adjust the tension of the yarn so that the grafted stitches look nice and even.

btw: Remember: On the lower needle, the order is purl, knit, off; on the upper needle, the order is knit, purl, off.

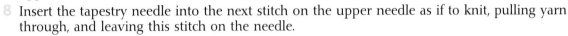

three-needle bind-off

You don't use a tapestry needle to do the three-needle bind-off—you knit and bind off stitches together, so it doesn't even feel like finishing. This technique is good for unshaped shoulders and other straight seams. As with Kitchener stitch, you need to have the same number of stitches on each piece. The setup goes like this: Have the two sets of live stitches each on a knitting needle, and have a third needle the same size as the other two. You can knit the seam with the working yarn if it's still attached, or you can start with a new strand of the same yarn you used to knit your pieces.

Don't be discouraged if you feel clumsy; you'll get the hang of it sooner or later, and you'll be glad you stuck with it. Here's how you do it:

1 Hold the needles with the stitches on them parallel in your left hand, with the right sides of your knitting facing each other.

2 Insert the tip of the third needle into the first stitch on the front needle as if to knit and then into the first stitch on the back needle as if to knit. Wrap the working yarn around the tip of the third needle as you would to knit.

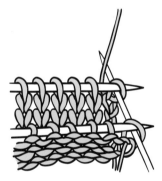

3 Bring the loop through the first stitch on the back needle, as you would to knit, and then bring the same loop all the way through to the front of the first stitch on the front needle as well.

4 Slip both old stitches off the parallel needles, just as you would to knit them. You should now have 1 stitch on the third needle.

5 Repeat steps 2–4 a second time. You should now have 2 stitches on the third needle.

6 Pass the first stitch on the third needle over the second stitch to bind off.

7 Continue knitting together the corresponding stitches from each needle and binding off as you go until only 1 stitch remains on the third needle. Cut the yarn, leaving a 6-inch tail, and pull the tail through the last stitch to secure.

8 Weave in the loose ends.

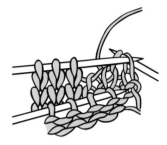

pick up stitches every which way

There's something deeply satisfying about picking up stitches, especially if you hate to sew seams. To think that you can just knit a row of stitches directly into your sweater, hat, bag—whatever—and start knitting! You commonly pick up stitches for things like button bands, neckbands, collars, or hoods. After you pick up the stitches along an edge, you knit them to create the thing you're adding. When you finish knitting the collar, button band, or whatever it is, you bind off, and voilà—it's done. No sewing. You can even pick up stitches along a straight armhole edge and knit a sleeve right onto a sweater.

The kind of edge you're picking up from determines how you pick up the stitches. For example, you can pick up along a straight vertical edge, like a cardigan front, to make a button band. Or you can pick up along a straight bound-off edge, like a pocket top, to add an edging. You can also pick up stitches around curved edges like necklines to knit on collars or neckbands.

btw: Generally, to pick up stitches, you use one of the needles you're going to knit the add-on with. Some instructions, however, call for a needle one or two sizes smaller.

picking up stitches along a horizontal edge

Here's how you pick up stitches along a horizontal—bound-off or cast-on—edge:

1 With the right side of your knitting facing, and working from right to left, insert the needle into the center of the V of the first stitch just below the bound-off or cast-on row.

2 Wrap the working yarn around the needle as you would to knit, leaving a 6-inch tail at the back.

3 Bring the loop of working yarn to the front, back through the stitch. You just picked up your first stitch!

4 Repeat steps 1–3 for each stitch across the edge.

btw: Here's a good rule of thumb for picking up stitches: Pick up 1 stitch for every stitch along a horizontal edge, and pick up approximately 3 stitches for every 4 rows along a vertical edge.

picking up stitches along a vertical edge

Picking up stitches along a vertical edge is similar to picking them up along a horizontal edge, except that instead of sticking the needle into the center of each stitch along the horizontal row, you insert the needle into the spaces between the first and second stitches all along the vertical row. Here's how you do it:

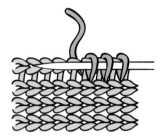

1 Turn your work so that the right side is facing and the vertical rows run horizontally.
2 Working from right to left, insert the needle from front to back into the space between the first and second stitches.
3 Wrap the working yarn around the needle as you would to knit, leaving a 6-inch tail at the back.
4 Bring the loop of working yarn to the front, back through the space where the needle went in. You just picked up your first stitch!
5 Repeat steps 2–4, skipping a row every few stitches, to account for the fact that there are more rows per inch than stitches per inch.

picking up stitches along a curved edge

Picking up stitches along a curved edge—like along neck shaping—consists of picking up stitches horizontally and vertically over the same edge. To do it, you follow these steps:

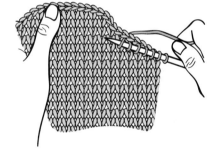

1 Working from right to left, with the right side facing, insert the needle into the center of the V of the first stitch, just below the bound-off edge of the shaping.
2 Wrap the working yarn around the needle, as you would to knit, leaving a 6-inch tail at the back.
3 Pick up all the stitches on the horizontal section of the shaping until you get to the vertical section.
4 Continue picking up stitches as you would for a vertical edge, skipping a row every few stitches, if necessary. Be sure not to insert the needle into any large holes caused by the shaping, as doing so will result in a hole in your picked-up edge.

Now you'll know what to do when your instructions say "pick up and knit *x* number of stitches."

Picking Up Stitches Evenly

Knitting instructions usually tell you to pick up a specific number of stitches evenly along an edge. When you have to pick up a lot of stitches over a long edge, this can be pretty tricky. If the stitches are not picked up evenly, the outcome can be a messy-looking border or neckband. You can save yourself the aggravation of having to redo your pick-up row over and over again by marking the pick-up edge at regular intervals. To do this, you place pins, spaced evenly apart, along the edge where the stitches are to be picked up. Then you figure out how many stitches should be picked up between the pins by dividing the total number of stitches to be picked up by the number of spaces between the pins.

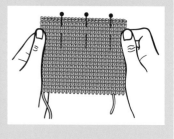

buttonholes

Making buttonholes is easy. If you can increase and decrease, you can make a buttonhole. There are quite a few ways to make buttonholes, probably because buttons come in so many different sizes. Here are two often-used buttonholes—the eyelet buttonhole and the one-row horizontal buttonhole—that should work for most situations. Just be sure the size of your buttonhole is right for your button.

eyelet buttonhole

The eyelet buttonhole is the easiest and most common buttonhole. It makes a small buttonhole with fine yarns and a smallish hole for chunkier yarns. Here's how you make one:

1 Work to the point where you want the buttonhole to be and then yo, k2tog; continue the row as before.

2 On the next row, work the yo as you would a regular stitch.

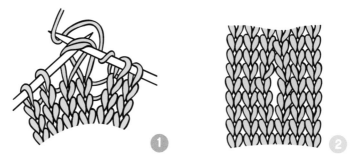

one-row horizontal buttonhole

A one-row horizontal buttonhole makes a nice neat buttonhole and is done in one row instead of two. You can adjust the size of the buttonhole by binding off fewer or more stitches. Here's the technique:

1 On the right side, work to the point where you want the buttonhole to start. Bring the yarn to the front, slip the next stitch from the left needle as if to purl, and bring the yarn to the back.

2 *Slip purlwise the next stitch from the left needle to the right and pass the first slipped stitch over it and off the needle. Repeat from * four times, keeping the yarn at the back the whole time. Slip the last bound-off stitch back to the left needle as shown. You have bound off 5 stitches.

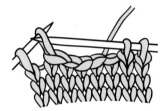

note: If you want a bigger buttonhole, bind off more stitches; for a smaller buttonhole, bind off 2, 3, or 4 stitches.

3 Turn your work so that the wrong side is facing and bring the yarn to the back.

4 Insert the right needle between the first and second stitches on the left needle and wrap the yarn around the right needle as if to knit. Bring the loop to the front as if to knit, but instead of slipping the old stitch off the left needle, use the right needle to place the new loop onto the left needle. You have used the cable cast-on method to cast on 1 stitch!

5 Repeat step 4 five times more. You have cast on 6 stitches.

note: If you bound off fewer or more stitches than 5, be sure to cast on the same number you bound off plus 1.

6 Turn the work back so that the right side is facing. Bring the yarn to the back and slip the first stitch from the left needle to the right needle; pass the additional cast-on stitch over the slipped stitch to close the buttonhole. Work to the end of the row as usual. Buttonhole accomplished!

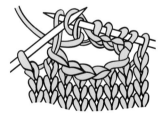

Finishing Buttonholes

If your buttonhole looks a little messy, as knit buttonholes often do, or if it's too loose for your button, you can neaten it up with buttonhole stitch, as shown here. You can use the same yarn you knit the project with; or, if you're very bold, you can use an accent color.

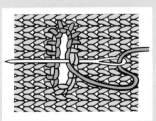

Chapter 9

fun stuff to decorate your knitting

If your hat looks bald or your scarf seems to be missing something, you can change all that with a little embellishment. Adding a pompom or tassel may be all you need to do to revamp that hat or scarf. Sometimes a little embroidered stitch running along the edge in an accent color is enough to transform a dull sweater into something really eye-catching.

This chapter shows you all kinds of fun stuff: fringe, pompoms, tassels, embroidery, and crochet trimmings. None of these delightful details are that hard to do, and another half hour can be all it takes to make over your knitting into something that is truly you.

fringe, tassels, and pompoms

Fringe, tassels, and pompoms are all made from bundles of cut yarn, but each has a completely different effect. You don't have to make any of these out of the same yarn you used to knit your project, so it's a good way to decorate your knitting *and* use up scrap yarn.

fringe

Fringe doesn't have to adorn scarves only. You can liven up a sweater hem or bag by attaching fringe, too. Fringe can use up quite a bit of yarn, so make sure you have a hefty supply so that your fringe doesn't look skimpy and straggly. You need fewer strands per bundle with thick yarn and more strands per bundle with thinner yarns. Experiment with different amounts and lengths on your gauge swatch if you want to be sure it's going to look good.

To make fringe, you need yarn, a pair of scissors, and a crochet hook. Then you follow these steps:

1 Decide how long you want your final fringe to be; cut yarn to double that length, plus an inch extra for the knot.

2 Hold the strands together, with the ends matched up, creating a loop at the top.

3 Hold your knitting with the wrong side facing you. Insert the crochet hook from front to back, just above the cast–on or bind–off row, take hold of your loop of folded strands, and pull it through the knitting from back to front.

4 Wrap the strands around the crochet hook and use it to pull the ends through the loop.

5 Pull on the ends to tighten the knot.

6 Repeat steps 2–5 across the cast–on or bind–off row to finish the fringe.

7 Trim the fringe to even it up.

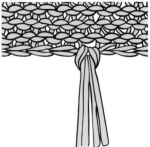

tassels

Long tassels add an elegant touch to cushion corners, scarf ends, and hat tops. Short and bristly tassels are more playful and fun looking—try sewing one or two at the top of a close–fitting hat. A tassel looks kind of like a large bundle of fringe, but they're not made the same way. To make a tassel, you need yarn, of course, a piece of rigid cardboard, scissors, and a tapestry needle. Here's how you make one:

1 Cut the cardboard into a rectangle that's about 3 inches by whatever length you want your tassel to be. (So, for a 5–inch tassel, you need a 3 x 5–inch rectangle of cardboard.)

2 Wrap the yarn around the cardboard about 40 times, or until you have the thickness you want. Very thin yarn requires more wraps; thicker yarns require fewer wraps.

3 Thread a tapestry needle with a 12–inch strand of the same yarn and insert the needle between the top of the cardboard and the wrapped strands. Pull it all the way through and tie the strand in a very tight knot.

4 Insert the scissors between the cardboard and the wrapped strands at the other end and cut the tassel free.

5 Cut a 10–inch strand of yarn and wrap it around the tassel a few times, about ½ inch down from the tied end; then tie the ends tightly in a knot. Conceal these yarn ends by threading them through a tapestry needle and inserting the needle back into the tassel near the top. Pull the needle out at the loose end of the tassel and cut the yarn to the same length as the rest of the tassel.

note: If you want your tassel to be more like a cheerleader pompom, you can skip step 5. You might want to give it a few more wraps for fullness before tying the top, though.

6 Trim the tassel to even it up, and use the tails at the top to sew the tassel to your knitting project.

pompoms

You can put pompoms on most anything—hat tops or brims (at the ears looks cute), scarf ends, sweater hems, mitten or sock cuffs, you name it. You can even use tight, round pompoms as buttons. Or you could sew together a whole bunch of pompoms for a no–knitting scarf!

There are two ways to make pompoms: You can make a relaxed, loose pompom using the same materials you use to make a tassel, or you can make a firm, round pompom using cardboard circles or a commercial pompom maker.

making a loose pompom

To make a loose pompom, you need a fair amount of yarn, a piece of rigid cardboard, scissors, and a tapestry needle. Here's how you do it:

1 Cut the piece of cardboard into a square that is the same width you want your pompom to be.

2 Wrap the yarn around the pompom about 40 to 60 times, depending on the thickness of the yarn. (If you're using multiple strands, you can wrap fewer times. For example, for a double strand, wrap 30 times.)

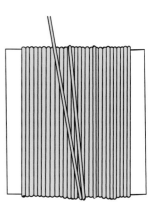

3 Carefully remove the cardboard from the wrapped yarn.

4 Wrap a 12–inch strand of yarn tightly around the center of the yarn loops twice and then tie it in a very tight knot.

5 Cut the loops and fluff up the pompom to even it out.

6 Use the tie ends to sew the pompom to your knitting.

btw: You can make a multicolored pompom by wrapping several yarns at once. Another cool accessory is a loopy pompom: You just skip cutting the ends.

To make a firm, round, velvety pompom, you need stiff cardboard, lots of yarn, a pair of scissors, and a tapestry needle. It's easy:

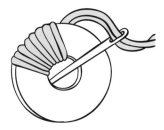

1　Cut two firm cardboard circles to about the same size you want your pompom to be. You can trace a glass, a can, or something circular that is the right size.

2　Trace and cut another circle directly in the center of each cardboard circle, about ¾ to 1 inch in diameter.

3　Match up the two cardboard pieces, one on top of the other, thread the yarn end through the tapestry needle, and use the needle to wrap the yarn around the circles tightly, densely, and evenly until the hole at the center is filled. Cut the yarn end.

4　Insert the scissors between the two circles and under the yarn. Cut the yarn all the way around the outside of the cardboard circles.

5　Bring a 12-inch strand of yarn between the two cardboard circles and around the center of the cut yarns. Tie it very tightly in a square knot.

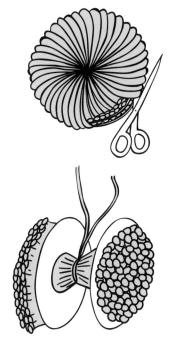

6　Remove the cardboard circles, fluff up the pompom, and use scissors to trim the pompom to a nice round shape.

7　Use the tie ends to sew the pompom to your knitting.

btw: If you like new craft toys, you can buy a set of plastic pompom makers. If you're a pompom fan, you won't regret this purchase!

stitching on your knitting

If you're an embroiderer, you can use what you know to decorate your knitting. If you don't already know embroidery stitches, you can use this section to learn a few fun ways to add color and cuteness to your knitting to make it even more personal. All you need is a tapestry needle and yarn in a few different colors. Be sure to embroider *after* you've blocked your project, or you might get some puckering. Embroidered stitches show up best on flat knitting, like stockinette stitch and garter stitch.

For all the embroidery stitches, thread your tapestry needle with the color yarn of your choice, leaving an unknotted tail, 6 inches or so long, coming out the eye. Tie a knot about 4 inches up from the long end, so you can weave in the end later.

straight stitch

You probably already know how to do straight stitch—you just weave the needle in and out, making straight stitches. It's easy and plain, yes, but straight stitch can really add a cute touch when worked around the perimeter of a sweater or bag, or when repeated around the circumference of a hat. It's also a good drawing stitch. Or why not use straight stitch to sew one of your old gauge swatches onto your knitting as a pocket? Here's how you do it:

1 Bring the needle up through the knitting from back to front, until the knot stops it.

2 Lay the needle flat with the knitting and insert it from front to back where you want the stitch end to be; in the same motion, reinsert the tip from underneath so that it comes back out the same stitch length from the second insertion. Pull the yarn all the way through.

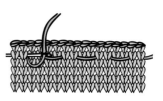

3 Continue weaving the needle in and out until you're finished.

4 End with the needle on the wrong side and weave in the ends.

whipstitch

Whipstitch is another easy one that you've probably already done without knowing what it was called. In a fun contrast color, a whipstitched edge can be all it takes to make a one-color project stand out. Here's what you do:

1 Bring the needle up through the knitting from back to front, until the knot stops it.

2 Bring the needle in and out from back to front up the side of the knitting until you're finished.

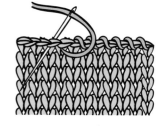

3 End with the needle on the wrong side and weave in the ends.

blanket stitch

Blanket stitch adds a rustic, homespun feeling when used on sweaters, blankets, and scarves. It also works well at concealing slightly uneven edges. Try it out:

1 Bring the needle through at the edge of your knitting from back to front, until the knot stops it.

2 Moving from right to left, insert the needle at the desired depth into the edge and bring it out again to the front, taking care that the needle tip overlaps the yarn coming out of the starting point.

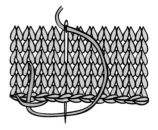

3 Repeat step 2 along the edge of your knitting.

4 End with the needle on the wrong side and weave in the ends.

duplicate stitch

Duplicate stitch, also known as *Swiss darning*, is a fun stitch that duplicates the knit stitch—the V—right on top of it in the knitting. You can use it to put motifs on your knitting that look like you knit them in. So if you want to put a skull, heart, or whatever on your knitting but can't be bothered with intarsia, then this is for you. You don't knot your yarn for this one. Here's how it works:

1 Bring the needle up through the knitting from back to front, at the hole just below the V that you want to duplicate. Pull the yarn through, leaving a 6-inch tail.

2 Insert the needle from right to left under both loops of the V above the stitch you want to duplicate; pull the yarn all the way through.

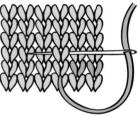

3 Reinsert the needle into the hole below your stitch—the same hole that the needle came through in step 1—and bring it out again below the next stitch to be worked, all in one movement.

4 Repeat steps 2 and 3 to create duplicate stitch.

5 End with the needle on the wrong side and weave in the ends.

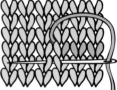

chain stitch

When worked in a row, chain stitch looks like a line of linked loops (a chain!). You can also draw with it for a playful look. Try it:

1 Bring the needle through the knitting from back to front, pulling the yarn through until the knot stops it.

2 Hold the yarn in a loop; reinsert the needle right next to where it came out in step 1; bring the needle back out over the loop a small stitch away.

3 Repeat step 2 to create chain stitch.

4 End with the needle on the wrong side and weave in the ends.

french knot

You can use French knots for a lot of things: in a row along a straight edge, scattered about like polka dots, or as the center of a lazy daisy. They take a little practice, so get started:

1 Bring the needle through the knitting from back to front, pulling the yarn through until the knot stops it.

2 Grasp the yarn about 1 inch above the point where it came out and wind the yarn around the tip of the needle two or three times, moving from the eye of the needle to the tip, as shown.

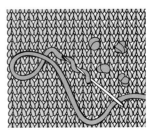

3   Still grasping the wound yarn, reinsert the needle right next to the point where it came out and pull it through all the way to the back to create the knot. Don't pull too hard, or you will pull the knot to the back of the work.

4   End with the needle on the wrong side and weave in the ends.

stem stitch

Stem stitch is good for outlining, and of course it makes a lovely stem for embroidered flowers. Try it:

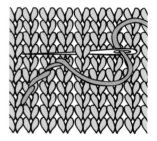

1   Bring the needle through the knitting from back to front, pulling the yarn through until the knot stops it.

2   Make a ¼-inch straight stitch to start.

3   Bring the needle through from back to front just next to the center of the stitch you made in step 2.

4   Hold the yarn with your left thumb above the point where it just came through and reinsert the needle about ¼ inch to the right of the first stitch, bringing the needle out at the end point of the first stitch.

5   Repeat step 4 until you are finished.

6   End with the needle on the wrong side and weave in the ends.

lazy daisy stitch

Lazy daisies are flowers made from a circle of chain stitches with a French knot at the center. You can adjust the size by making your chain stitches smaller or larger.

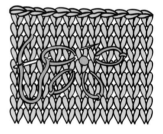

1   Work one chain stitch (see page 77), but instead of bringing the needle back into the stitch, insert it just below the loop of the chain, bringing it back out to the front at the other end of the chain, as shown here. That's your first petal.

2   Repeat step 1 in a circle, until you have completed the daisy.

3   End with the needle on the wrong side and weave in the ends.

4   Work a French knot at the center of the ring of petals.

crochet chains and edgings

Don't worry, you don't have to learn all there is to know about crochet, but it's a good idea to get just a few crochet essentials under your belt so that you can spruce up your knitting even more. If you have a project with messy edges, a row of single crochet can neaten it up. What's more, a picot crochet trim turns a boring scarf, hat, or bag into something fun and frilly. If crochet edgings are too much for you just now, at least take a look at how to make a crochet chain; crochet chains make terrific ties for tassels, pompoms, and hats.

You'll need yarn and an appropriately sized crochet hook.

btw: Crochet hooks are numbered similarly to knitting needles. Look for a crochet hook that's the same number of millimeters in diameter as your knitting needles. For example, if you're using 5 mm (US 8) knitting needles for your knitting, you need a 5 mm (US H-8) crochet hook for the edging.

crochet a chain

Chain stitch in crochet is like casting on in knitting: It's the foundation row of stitches that you work from. When you crochet directly onto your knitting, you don't need to crochet a chain first. However, it's still good to know how to crochet a chain because you can crochet chains as button loops, as ornamental cords, and as one of the elements of a picot crochet edge. Here's how you make a chain:

1 Make a slipknot, leaving a 6–inch tail. Insert the crochet hook into the slipknot.
2 Wrap the working yarn around the crochet hook from back to front (creating a yarn over loop) so that the hook catches the yarn.
3 Holding the working yarn in your left hand and the hook in your right, pull the yarn over loop on the hook through the slipknot. You have made 1 chain! This is called "chain 1" or "ch 1" in crochet lingo.
4 Repeat steps 2 and 3 until the chain is the desired length. Cut the yarn, leaving a 6–inch tail, and pull it snugly through the last loop to finish the chain.

slip stitch crochet edging

A slipstitch crochet edging by itself provides a firm, neat border. You can also use it under a row of single crochet for a more substantial trim. Try it:

1 Insert the hook into the edge of your knitting at the right corner.
2 Loop the yarn around the hook (yarn over) and pull the loop through to the front.
3 Insert the crochet hook into the next stitch of the knitting, yarn over again, and pull the loop through both the knitting and the loop on the hook from step 1. You should have 1 loop remaining on the hook.
4 Repeat step 3 across the edge. Cut the yarn and pull it snugly through the last loop to finish.

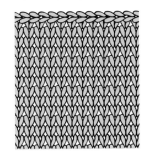

single crochet edging

A single crochet edging looks somewhat similar to a slipstitch crochet edge, but it's a little meatier. Like the other crochet edgings shown here, it's worked from right to left. Here's how it goes:

1 Insert the hook into the edge of your knitting at the right corner.
2 Loop the yarn around the hook (yarn over) and pull the loop through to the front.
3 Working from the front, yarn over and pull a new loop through the first loop.
4 Insert the hook into the next stitch to the left on the knitting, yarn over, and pull a new loop through. You now have 2 loops on the hook.

5 Yarn over the crochet hook again and pull this new loop through both loops already on the hook. You now have 1 loop on the hook.
6 Repeat steps 4 and 5 across the edge. Cut the yarn and pull it through the last loop to finish the edging.

picot crochet edging

If you've managed the last two edgings, then this one won't be difficult, and look how great it is. You can add this fun touch to your knitting in a matter of minutes. See for yourself:

1 Insert the hook into the edge of your knitting at the right corner.
2 Work 1 single crochet (see "Single Crochet Edging," above).
3 Chain 3—or 4 or 5 if you want a chunkier picot (see "Crochet a Chain," page 79).
4 Insert the crochet hook back into the same stitch, yarn over, and bring up a loop.
5 Yarn over again and pull the loop through both loops on the hook.
6 Single crochet 2 (into the next 2 stitches, moving left).
7 Repeat steps 2–5 across the edge. Cut the yarn and pull it through the last loop to finish the edging.

part 2

your style, your projects

1. When you walk into a clothing store, you:
   a. Make a beeline for the black clothing.
   b. Look at the mannequins' outfits to see what the latest trends are.
   c. Check out the dangly earrings and funky bags.
   d. Head for the khaki minis and gingham shirts.
   e. It depends on the day.

2. If you were a dessert, you would most likely be:
   a. A black-and-white cookie.
   b. Single-origin dark chocolate truffles.
   c. Fruit with granola sprinkled on top.
   d. Apple pie a la mode.
   e. It depends on the day.

3. Your room is most like:
   a. A shrine to your favorite punk band.
   b. An interior decorator's showplace.
   c. An artist's studio.
   d. A sporting goods store.
   e. It depends on the day.

4. Your favorite colors to wear are:
   a. Black.
   b. Whatever is "in" right now.
   c. Lots of different colors and patterns at the same time.
   d. Pastels and neutrals.
   e. It depends on the day.

5. Your dream boyfriend wears:
   a. Skinny black jeans, a studded belt, and a Ramones T-shirt.
   b. Only the best names in fashion.
   c. Jeans with paint splattered on them.
   d. Cargo shorts and a polo shirt.
   e. It depends on the day.

if you answered:

Mostly a's: You are definitely into the punk look. Knitting is for all kinds of people, and there are a lot of women rockers who knit while they're hanging out backstage. You can check out the skull wristbands on page 134, or how about the mini kilt (adorn it with safety pins) on page 139? It looks great with striped tights and platform combat boots.

Mostly b's: You are a fashionista! You love designer clothes, high fashion, and elegant apparel. Since you read all the fashion mags, you know that a lot of top models and celebs are knitting–addicted, just like you. Some perfect projects for you are the ruffled mini on page 126 and the stole on page 131. You'll also like the girly–girl stuff in Chapter 13.

Mostly c's: Do you consider yourself an artist? You like the funky, arty—maybe even hippie—style. You have a sensitive eye and can combine styles and colors to create a one–of–a–kind look. You have probably always been a crafty type, so knitting is right up your alley. You'll probably want to knit *lots* of things, but why not take a peek at the newsboy cap on page 85 or the "suede" bag on page 157?

Mostly d's: You preppy, you! You love gingham, pastel colors, and anything suitable for the yacht club. Good thing there are so many cute styles out there now to make preppy fun. In between tennis lessons, you'll want to chill out and knit the cute sleeveless hoodie on page 148, the cinch–top hat on page 146, or the pompom tennis socks on page 143.

Mostly e's: You refuse to be categorized, but you have this book, so you must like to knit! You will probably enjoy knitting the cozy mittens on page 99 or a warm comfy scarf (see page 121 and page 153). Or how about the funky little phone/MP3 player sweater on page 101?

An even mix of a's, b's, c's, and d's: Your style is most definitely eclectic! You're lucky because you'll probably want to knit everything in the book.

arty and funky

Cool and bohemian, you look like you don't care *too* much about your clothes—but you like to have a few special accessories that set you apart. Here are a few knit-ables you might like: A funky hat, extra-long arm warmers, and a long openwork belt, all adorned with vintage buttons and buckles. Be sure to embellish, embroider, and bejewel your projects to make them uniquely you.

Sweater-less Sleeves

Skill Level – Easy ◯ *Designer – Sharon Turner*

Arm apparel like this keeps you warm and lets you show off your shoulders at the same time. You can adjust the length to suit your taste. If you make the sleeves extra long, you can bunch them up around your elbows or let them slip down over the back of your hand. This pair is knit in the round (no seams!) in broken rib, which is actually reversible, so if you don't embroider the lazy daisy, you've got 2-in-1 arm warmers.

specifications

Size

S (M, L)

Size shown: M

Finished Measurements

Circumference: 5¾ (6½, 7½) inches

Length: 13 (14, 15) inches

Materials

- ◌ 1 skein Cascade Yarns *220 Quatro* (100% wool, 220 yd./100 g skein) color #9433
- ◌ US 7 (4.5 mm) double-pointed needles, set of 4
- ◌ Split-ring stitch marker
- ◌ Tapestry needle
- ◌ 2 yd. scrap yarn for lazy daisy, if desired
- ◌ 2 small buttons for daisy centers, if desired (the sample uses tiny vintage dome buttons)

Gauge

22 sts and 28 rnds to 4 inches in broken rib patt on US 7 (4.5 mm) needles, or size needed to obtain gauge

Pattern Stitches

Broken Rib (Mult of 2 Sts)

Rnd 1: *K1, p1; rep from * to end of rnd.

Rnd 2: Knit.

Rep rnds 1 and 2 for broken rib.

instructions

Using the long-tail cast-on method (see page 13) and double-pointed needle, CO 32 (36, 42) sts. Divide sts as evenly as possible over 3 dpns. Place split-ring marker in first st to note beginning of rnd and join round, being careful not to twist sts.

Work broken rib patt until sleeve measures 13 (14, 15) inches from beg, ending with rnd 1. Loosely BO all sts knitwise.

Finishing

Weave in ends.

Lightly block sleeves, if desired, and if your yarn's care instructions allow, using the instructions on pages 60–62.

Use tapestry needle and scrap yarn to embroider a 2-inch lazy daisy onto each sleeve, if desired. (See page 78 for lazy daisy instructions.) Weave in scrap yarn ends. Sew buttons to daisy centers.

Variation

You can easily make these into wrist warmers. Don't knit them as long (8 inches or so should do it) and add a one-row buttonhole (see page 70) for the thumb to come through when you're about 2 inches away from binding off. Begin the buttonhole after working the first 2 stitches of the round in the rib pattern and work it over 6–8 stitches, depending on the size of your thumb, and then continue the round in rib to the end. Finish from here as usual.

Newsboy Cap

Skill Level – Intermediate  *Designer – Sharon Turner*

Instead of buying one of those mass-produced newsboy caps from a street vendor or spending a fortune for one at an exclusive boutique, knit your own! It takes only a couple of nights to finish, and you need just one hank of yarn. The yarn used here has subtle color changes built in, but a one-color yarn would look terrific, too. The main part of the hat is worked in the round, so you don't have to sew a seam at the back. The brim is worked separately on straight needles, lined with lightweight interfacing, and then sewn on. If you can't get to a sewing or craft store for interfacing, don't worry—the reinforcement is nice but not necessary.

specifications

Size

One size

Finished Measurements

Circumference at brim: 20 inches

Materials

- 1 hank Noro *Kochoran* (50% wool/30% angora/20% silk, 175 yd./100 g hank) color #36
- US 10 (6 mm) double-pointed needles, set of 4 or 5
- US 10 (6 mm) straight needles
- Split-ring stitch markers
- Tapestry needle
- 1½-inch button for hat top, if desired
- 10 x 3-inch rectangle of light interfacing, for lining brim, if desired

Gauge

16 sts and 24 rnds to 4 inches in stockinette st on US 10 (6 mm) needles, or size needed to obtain gauge

Pattern Stitches

St st (Stockinette Stitch) Worked in Rnds

Knit every rnd.

St st (Stockinette Stitch) Worked in Rows

Row 1 (RS): Knit.

Row 2 (WS): Purl.

Rep rows 1 and 2 for St st worked in rows.

kfb (Knit into Front and Back)

Increase 1 st by knitting into the front and then into the back of the next st.

k2tog (Knit 2 Together)

Insert the right needle into the front of the next 2 sts on the left needle as if to knit. Wrap the yarn over the right needle and knit the 2 sts as 1 st.

p2tog (Purl 2 Together)

Insert the right needle into the front of the next 2 sts on the left needle as if to purl. Wrap the yarn over the right needle and purl the 2 sts as 1 st.

instructions

Using the long-tail cast-on method (see page 13) and double-pointed needles, CO 80 sts. Divide sts as evenly as possible over 3 or 4 dpns. Place split-ring marker in first st to note beginning of rnd, and join rnd, being careful not to twist sts.

Knit 1 rnd.

Purl 1 rnd.

Lower Body of Hat Shaping

Next rnd: *K9, kfb; rep from * to end—88 sts.

Knit 3 rnds.

Purl 1 rnd.

Next rnd: *K10, kfb; rep from * to end—96 sts.

Knit 3 rnds.

Purl 1 rnd.

Next rnd: *K11, kfb; rep from * to end—104 sts.

Knit 3 rnds.

Purl 1 rnd.

Center Body of Hat

Knit 4 rnds.

Purl 1 rnd.

Rep last 5 rnds 2 times more.

Top of Hat Shaping

Rnd 1: *K6, k2tog; rep from * to end—91 sts.

Rnd 2 and all other even-numbered rnds: Knit.

Rnd 3: *K5, k2tog; rep from * to end—78 sts.

Next rnd 5: *P4, p2tog; rep from * to end—65 sts.

Next rnd 7: *K3, k2tog; rep from * to end—52 sts.

Next rnd 9: *K2, k2tog; rep from * to end—39 sts.

Next rnd 11: *K1, k2tog; rep from * to end—26 sts.

Next rnd 13: *K2tog; rep from * to end—13 sts.

Knit 1 rnd.

Cut yarn, leaving a 10-inch tail, and pull through rem 13 sts; tighten.

Brim

At this point, you are done working in the round. Using straight needles, CO 3 sts.

Row 1 and all other WS rows: Purl.

Row 2 (RS): Kfb twice, k1—5 sts.

Row 4: K1, kfb twice, k2—7 sts.

Row 6: K2, kfb twice, k3—9 sts.

Row 8: K3, kfb twice, k4—11 sts.

Row 10: K4, kfb twice, k5—13 sts.

Row 12: K5, kfb twice, k6—15 sts.

Row 14: K6, kfb twice, k7—17 sts.

Row 16: K7, kfb twice, k8—19 sts.

Beg with a purl row, work in St st without further shaping until piece measures 5½ inches from beg, ending with a WS (purl) row. Place split-ring markers before and after the center st to mark it.

Next row (RS): K7, k2tog, k1 (center axis st), k2tog, k7—17 sts.

Next row and all rem WS rows: Purl.

Next row: K6, k2tog, k1 (center axis st), k2tog, k6—15 sts.

Continue as established, dec 1 st before and after the center axis st on every RS row, until 5 sts rem, ending with a WS row.

Next row (RS): K2tog, k1, k2tog—3 sts.

Purl 1 row.

Cut yarn, leaving a 20-inch tail, and pull through rem 3 sts; tighten.

Finishing

The brim will automatically fold along the axis st, with the WS inside. Steam brim to reduce curling.

Optional: If lining brim with interfacing, trace outline of brim onto interfacing. Cut out brim-shaped piece from interfacing, trimming down so that it fits inside the brim, between the wrong sides.

Pin double edge of brim along the cast-on edge of the hat and use the 20-inch tail to whipstitch it on (see page 76).

Weave in ends. Sew button to top of hat, if desired.

Variation

If the newsboy look is not for you, make this hat without the sewn-on brim for an easy tam. For an even more striking chapeau, work an extra 5 pattern rounds at the center body (that is, change the instructions under "Center Body of Hat" from "Rep last 5 rounds 2 times more" to "Rep last 5 rounds 3 times more"), and sew a huge fluffy pompom onto the top.

Hip Hip Belt

Skill Level – Intermediate 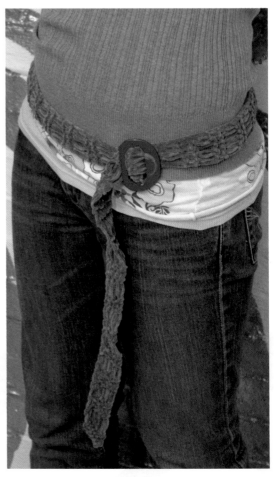 *Designer – Sharon Turner*

This belt is a cinch to make and looks great around the hip over billowy tops, dresses, or extra-long tank tops. Have fun searching for an old bakelite buckle like this one online or at thrift shops and vintage clothing stores. Or see if you can find something cool at a craft store. If you don't use the "suede" yarn, be sure to choose something that will hold up well, like cotton, linen, or hemp; ribbon yarn or tape yarn would be great substitutes, too.

specifications

Size

One size

Finished Measurements

Length: 37 inches or desired length

Materials

- 1 skein Lion Brand *Lion Suede* (100% polyester, 122 yd./85 g skein) color #177
- US 9 (5.5 mm) straight needles
- Tapestry needle
- Belt buckle to accommodate a 2-inch-wide belt

Gauge

16 sts and 12 rows to 4 inches in drop stitch on US 9 (5.5 mm) needles, or size needed to obtain gauge

Pattern Stitches

yo (Yarn Over)

Bring the working yarn to the front of the needles and lay it over the right needle from front to back. This creates another stitch.

Drop Stitch (Any Number of Sts)

Rows 1 and 2: Knit.

Row 3 (RS): K1, *yo twice, k1; rep from * to end.

Row 4: K1, *drop 2 yarn overs, k1; rep from * to end.

Rep rows 1–4 for drop stitch.

note: To drop the 2 yarn overs, you slip them off the left needle without working them.

instructions

Using the long–tail cast–on method (see page 13), CO 6 sts.

Work in drop stitch until belt measures 37 inches, or desired length, ending with row 1 of patt. BO knitwise, leaving a 10–inch tail.

Finishing

Fold one end of the belt around the center shaft of the belt buckle and firmly stitch in place. You can use the tail left from binding off to do this. Weave in ends.

Variation

If you're not a belt wearer, make this into a scarf instead. Use a nice soft yarn (that your neck can tolerate) in the same gauge and cast on 12 or more stitches, depending on how wide you want your scarf to be. Then work it to the desired length. Nearly instant scarf!

Chapter 11
tomboy

Tomboy may not be the right word to describe your style, but whatever it is, you don't like to wear fussy, girly stuff—not every day anyway. You like to be comfortable; and your clothes should allow you the freedom to hop on your bike or skateboard or plop down on the grass without worry.

If this description fits you, you'll love the projects in this chapter: The cozy thermal has the look of your favorite everyday thermal tee, but it's knit in super-warm and soft alpaca so you can wear it *over* your tee for extra warmth during the fall and winter. The striped skate cap keeps your head warm and looks cool at the same time, and it's easy to knit. You'll probably want to make several in different color schemes. The chunky mittens knit up in no time and look great hanging out of your thermal sweater or coat sleeves. And be sure to dress your phone or MP3 player in the little striped sweater at the end of the chapter.

Skate Cap

Skill Level – Easy   *Designer – Kitty Wilson Jarrett*

When you want to pass as one of the boys, pull on this warm striped cap. For a tight, skull cap fit, make the small size; for a roomier hat that covers your ears, make the large size. This quick and easy hat gives you practice knitting in the round and making stripes. It also shows you how to use two kinds of decreases: one that slants to the right (k2tog), and one that slants to the left (ssk). You use these two decreases together to form the cornered top of the hat.

specifications

Size

S (L)

Size shown: L

Finished Measurements

Circumference: 18 (19) inches

Materials

- 1 ball elann.com *Pamir* (80% wool/20% mohair, 81 yd./50 g ball) color #680 (A), 1 ball color #473 (B), and 1 ball color #517 (C)
- US 5 (3.75 mm) 16-inch circular needle
- US 6 (4 mm) 16-inch circular needle
- US 6 (4 mm) double-pointed needles, set of 5
- 4 stitch markers
- Tapestry needle

Gauge

18 sts and 26 rows to 4 inches in stockinette st on US 6 (4 mm) needles, or size needed to obtain gauge

Pattern Stitches

St st (Stockinette Stitch) Worked in Rnds

Knit every rnd.

2 x 2 Rib (Mult of 4 Sts) Worked in Rnds

Rnd 1: *K2, p2; rep from * to end of rnd.

Rep rnd 1 for 2 x 2 rib worked in rnds

k2tog (Knit 2 Together)

Insert the right needle into the front of the next 2 sts on the left needle as if to knit. Wrap the yarn over the right needle and knit the 2 sts as 1 st.

ssk (Slip, Slip, Knit)

Insert the right needle from front to back into the front of the next st on the left needle and slip it onto the right needle. Rep this with the next st. (You have slipped 2 sts knitwise from the left needle to the right needle.) Insert the left needle into the fronts of both slipped sts and then knit them as 1 st.

instructions

With smaller needle and A, use the long-tail method (see page 13) to CO 84 (88) sts. Place marker to to note the beginning of the rnd and join sts in a circle, being careful not to twist sts.

Knit 2 rnds.

Continuing with A, work in 2 x 2 rib as follows:

Rnd 1: *K2, p2; rep from * to end of rnd.

Rep this rnd 4 (5) times more.

Change to larger circular needle and, continuing with A, knit 4 rnds. Do not cut A.

Join B and knit 2 rnds. Cut B, leaving a 6-inch tail.

Knit 1 rnd in A. Cut A, leaving a 6-inch tail.

Join C and knit 4 rnds. Cut C, leaving a 6-inch tail.

Join A and knit 1 rnd. Do not cut A.

Join B and knit 2 rnds. Cut B, leaving a 6-inch tail.

Continuing with A only, knit every rnd until hat measures 4½ (5¼) inches from CO edge.

Next rnd: *K21 (22); place marker, rep from * to end—4 markers placed.

note: Use a marker of a unique color for the first marker so you can easily tell where the rnd begins.

Top Decreases

note: When too few sts rem to continue on the circular needle, change to a set of 5 dpns. Place the sts from between the first and second markers on one needle, the sts from between the second and third markers on a second needle, and so on.

Rnd 1: *K2tog, k17 (18), ssk; rep from * to end—76 (80) sts.

Rnds 2, 4, 6, 8, and 10: Knit.

Rnd 3: *K2tog, k15 (16), ssk; rep from * to end—68 (72) sts.

Rnd 5: *K2tog, k13 (14), ssk; rep from * to end—60 (64) sts.

Rnd 7: *K2tog, k11 (12), ssk; rep from * to end—52 (56) sts.

Rnd 9: *K2tog, k9 (10), ssk; rep from * to end—44 (48) sts.

Rnd 11: *K2tog, k7 (8), ssk; rep from * to end—36 (40) sts.

Rnd 12: *K2tog, k5 (6), ssk; rep from * to end—28 (32) sts.

Rnd 13: *K2tog, k3 (4), ssk; rep from * to end—20 (24) sts.

Rnd 14: *K2tog, k1 (2), ssk; rep from * to end—12 (16) sts.

For size S, go to the finishing instructions. For size L, complete another dec rnd, as follows:

Rnd 15 (size L only): *K2tog, ssk; rep from * to end—8 sts.

Finishing

Cut yarn, leaving a 6-inch tail, and thread tail through rem 12 (8) sts to close top of hat.

Weave in ends.

Block cap, if desired, and if your yarn's care instructions allow, using the instructions on pages 60–62.

Cozy Thermal Sweater

Skill Level – Intermediate  **Designer – Jill Draper**

This sweater will take you from the days that are just starting to get cold through the falling snow of winter months. The alpaca makes a light but warm garment that's perfect for keeping warm without a lot of bulky layers. With an easy unfinished collar and reverse seaming on the shoulders and around the armholes, it looks great with comfy cords or jeans and your favorite boots. The waffle stitch allows for a fitted look without any shaping. This is a fairly easy pattern, started in the round and broken into front and back at the armholes. A little crochet around the button band, a couple of seams, and it's ready to wear without a lot of fussy finishing. Covered buttons were used here, but this sweater would look equally great with leather or wood buttons.

specifications

Size

S (M, L, XL)

Size shown: S

Finished Measurements

Chest circumference: 32 (35, 38, 41) inches

note: These measurements are unblocked and slightly stretched; all sizes can be blocked to up to 2 inches larger around the chest.

Length: 23 (24, 25, 26) inches

Materials

- 7 (8, 9, 9) hanks Cascade Yarns *Baby Alpaca Chunky* (100% baby alpaca, 108 yd./100 g hank) color #550 (MC) and 1 hank color #566 (CC)
- US 10 (6 mm) 24–inch circular needle
- US 10 (6 mm) straight needles for working sleeves, if desired
- Large stitch holder
- Stitch markers
- Tapestry needle
- US H (5 mm) crochet hook
- 4 ⅞–inch buttons

Gauge

16 sts and 22 rows to 4 inches in waffle stitch (slightly stretched) on US 10 (6 mm) needles, or size needed to obtain gauge

Pattern Stitches

3 x 1 Rib (Mult of 4 Sts) Worked in Rnds

Rnd 1: *K3, p1; rep from * to end.

Rep rnd 1 for 3 x 1 rib worked in rnds.

3 x 1 Rib (Mult of 4 Sts) Worked in Rows

Row 1 (RS): k1, *k3, p1; rep from * to last st, k1.

Row 2 (WS): p1, *k1, p3; rep from * to last st, p1.

Rep rows 1 and 2 for 3 x 1 rib worked in rows.

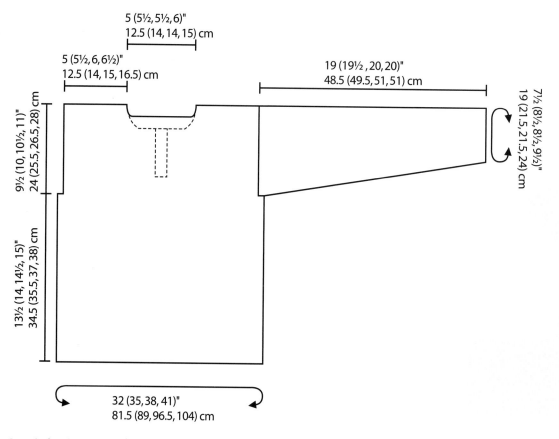

5 (5½, 5½, 6)"
12.5 (14, 14, 15) cm

5 (5½, 6, 6½)"
12.5 (14, 15, 16.5) cm

19 (19½, 20, 20)"
48.5 (49.5, 51, 51) cm

7½ (8½, 8½, 9½)"
19 (21.5, 21.5, 24) cm

9½ (10, 10½, 11)"
24 (25.5, 26.5, 28) cm

13½ (14, 14½, 15)"
34.5 (35.5, 37, 38) cm

32 (35, 38, 41)"
81.5 (89, 96.5, 104) cm

Waffle Stitch (Mult of 4 Sts) Worked in Rnds

Rnds 1–4: *K3, p1; rep from * to end.

Rnd 5: Purl.

Rep rnds 1–5 for waffle stitch worked in rnds.

Waffle Stitch (Mult of 4 Sts) Worked in Rows

Rows 1 and 3 (RS): *K3, p1; rep from * to end.

Rows 2 and 4 (WS): *K1, p3; rep from * to end.

Row 5: Purl.

Rows 6 and 8: Rep row 2.

Rows 7 and 9: Rep row 1.

Row 10: Knit.

Rep rows 1–10 for waffle stitch worked in rows.

k2tog (Knit 2 Together)

Insert the right needle into the front of the next 2 sts on the left needle as if to knit. Wrap the yarn over the right needle and knit the 2 sts as 1 st.

p2tog (Purl 2 Together)

Insert the right needle into the front of the next 2 sts on the left needle as if to purl. Wrap the yarn over the right needle and purl the 2 sts as 1 st.

Make Buttonhole

Row 1: Maintaining patt, work to where you want the buttonhole to be, BO 2 sts, work in patt to end.

Row 2: Work in patt to where sts were bound off on previous row. Using backward-loop method (see page 13), CO 2 sts, work in patt to end.

Seed Stitch (Mult of 2 Sts) Worked in Rows

Row 1: *P1, k1; rep from * to end.

Row 2: *K1, p1; rep from * to end.

Rep rows 1–2 for seed stitch worked in rows.

m1 (Make 1)

Increase 1 st by using the left needle to pick up the horizontal strand from front to back between the last st worked on the right needle and the next st to be worked on the left needle and knit into the picked–up strand.

instructions

Body

note: The body is worked in the round up to the armholes, and then it is worked back and forth in rows.

With circular needle and MC, use the long–tail cast-on method (see page 13) to CO 128 (140, 152, 164) sts. Place marker after 64th (70th, 76th, 82nd) st for side seam. Place marker to note beginning of rnd and second side seam. Join sts in a circle, being careful not to twist sts.

Body Ribbing

Work 3 x 1 rib as follows:

Rnd 1: *K3, p1; rep from * to end.

Rep this rnd 4 times more. Do not cut MC.

Next rnd: Join CC and work in 3 x 1 rib as established. Do not cut CC.

Next rnd: Change to MC and work 3 x 1 rib as established. Do not cut MC.

note: When switching colors, twist new yarn over old yarn to avoid holes.

Next rnd: Change to CC and work in 3 x 1 rib. Cut CC, leaving a 6-inch tail.

Next rnd: Change to MC and work 3 x 1 rib. Rep this rnd 2 times more.

Body Waffle Stitch

Work in waffle stitch, beg with rnd 1, until sweater body measures 13½ (14, 14½, 15) inches from CO edge.

Divide Front and Back

Next rnd: BO 2 (2, 3, 3) sts in patt, work in patt to 2 (2, 3, 3) sts before next marker, BO 2 (2, 3, 3) sts, remove marker, BO 2 (2, 3, 3) sts, work to end of rnd—122 (134, 143, 155) sts [60 (66, 70, 76) sts for front; 62 (68, 73, 79) sts for back].

Place front (the side no working yarn is currently attached to) onto large holder or waste yarn.

Sweater Back Armhole Shaping

Begin working back and forth in rows on back only, as follows:

Row 1 (WS): BO 2 (2, 3, 3) sts, work across row in established patt, now using waffle stitch as directed for rows—60 (66, 70, 76) sts.

Continue working in patt without further shaping until back measures 8½ (9, 9½, 10) inches from beg of armhole, ending with a WS row.

Sweater Back Neck Shaping

Next row (RS): Work in patt across 22 (24, 26, 28) sts, BO center 16 (18, 18, 20) sts for neck, work in patt across rem 22 (24, 26, 28) sts.

Next row: Work in patt across first shoulder; join second ball of yarn to second shoulder, and work in patt to end.

You will now work both shoulders at the same time, with two separate balls of yarn.

Next row (RS): Work in patt, dec 1 st at each neck edge, 1 st in from the edge—21 (23, 25, 27) sts for each shoulder.

note: Be sure to work your decreases so that the waffle stitch pattern is maintained. For example, if the row begins with k3, p1, you work the decrease as k2tog, p1. If the decrease row is the purl row, you p2tog for the decrease: p1, p2tog, purl to last 3 sts, p2tog, p1.

Next row (WS): Work even in patt.

Next row: Work as for previous RS row, dec 1 st at each neck edge, 1 st in from the edge—20 (22, 24, 26) sts for each shoulder.

BO both sets of shoulder sts in patt.

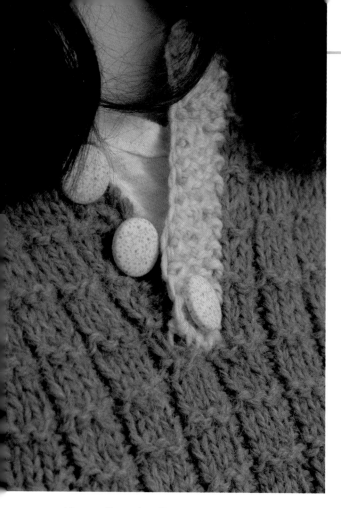

Place rem 32 (35, 37, 40) sts for right upper front onto stitch holder for later.

You will now work on the left front only.

> **Next row (WS):** With CC, (k1, p1) twice; change to MC, twisting yarns to prevent holes, and work in waffle stitch as established to end.
>
> **Next row (RS):** With MC, work in waffle stitch across 28 (31, 33, 36) sts; change to CC and (p1, k1) twice.

Continue as established, working buttonhole band in CC and seed stitch and body in MC and waffle stitch, until buttonhole band measures ½ inch, ending with a WS row.

> **Next row—work buttonhole (RS):** Work in patt to buttonhole band, change to CC, p1, BO 2, k1.
>
> **Next row—finish buttonhole (WS):** With CC, k1, use backward–loop method (see page 13) to CO 2 sts, p1, change to MC, and work in waffle stitch to end.

Continue working buttonhole band in seed stitch and body in waffle stitch, making 3 more buttonholes—1½ inches above the first and every 1½ inches after that, until you have completed 4 buttonholes total.

Work even in both stitch patts and colors as established until piece measures 5¾ (5¾, 6, 6) inches from beg of armhole, ending with a RS row.

Left Front Neck Shaping

> **Next row (WS):** Using CC, BO 4 button band sts in patt, change to MC, and BO 4 (5, 5, 6) sts in patt, work in patt to end—24 (26, 28, 30) sts. Cut CC, leaving a 6-inch tail.
>
> **Next row:** Work in patt to last 3 sts, dec 1 st, work rem st—23 (25, 27, 29) sts.
>
> **Next row:** Work 1 st, dec 1 st, work in patt to end—22 (24, 26, 28) sts.

Rep the last 2 rows once—20 (22, 24, 26) sts.

Work without further shaping until left front measures same as back. BO 20 (22, 24, 26) sts in patt.

Upper Sweater Front

Slip the 60 (66, 70, 76) sweater front sts onto a needle. With WS of sweater front facing, rejoin yarn to work front.

Work in waffle stitch as established, beginning with the correct WS row, until sweater measures 1¾ (1¾, 2, 2) inches from beginning of armhole, ending with a WS row.

Buttonhole Band

> **Next row (RS):** Work 28 (31, 33, 36) sts in patt, join CC, with CC CO 4 sts using backward–loop method (see page 13)—32 (35, 37, 40) sts for left upper front.

note: The 4 new sts form the buttonhole band and are worked in CC. Be sure to twist new yarn over old yarn when switching colors to prevent holes.

Upper Right Front

note: The button band is worked in MC.

Slip the 32 (35, 37, 40) right front sts from holder onto needle. Rejoin MC to right front with RS facing and work as follows:

Row 1 (RS): (P1, k1) twice for button band, work across rem 28 (31, 33, 36) sts in waffle stitch, as established.

Row 2 (WS): Work in waffle stitch to last 4 sts, (k1, p1) twice.

Rep rows 1 and 2 until right front measures 5¾ (5¾, 6, 6) inches from beginning of armhole, ending with a WS row.

Right Front Neck Shaping

Next row (RS): BO 8 (9, 9, 10) sts, work in patt to end—24 (26, 28, 30) sts.

Next row: Work 1 st, dec 1 st, work in patt to end—23 (25, 27, 29) sts.

Next row: Work in patt to last 3 sts, dec 1 st, work rem st—22 (24, 26, 28) sts.

Rep the last 2 rows once—20 (22, 24, 26) sts.

Work without further shaping until right front measures same as left front and back, ending on the same row of patt as for left front. BO rem 20 (22, 24, 26) sts in patt.

Sleeves

note: The sleeves are worked back and forth in rows.

Using MC and straight or circular needle and the long-tail cast-on method (see page 13), CO 30 (34, 34, 38) sts.

Sleeve Ribbing

Work 3 x 1 rib as follows:

Row 1 (RS): K1, *k3, p1; rep from * to last st, k1.
Row 2 (WS): P1, *k1, p3; rep from * to last st, p1.

Rep rows 1 and 2 once more, then row 1 once (5 rows total). Cut MC, leaving a 6–inch tail.

Next row (WS): Join CC and work 3 x 1 rib as established. Cut CC, leaving a 6–inch tail.

Next row (RS): Join MC and work 3 x 1 rib as established.

Rep last 2 rows once more.

Continue with MC in established 3 x 1 rib patt for 3 more rows.

Next row (RS): P1, m1, purl to last st, m1, p1—32 (36, 36, 40) sts.

Sleeve Waffle Stitch

Row 1 (WS): P2, *k1, p3; rep from * to last 2 sts, k1, p1.
Row 2 (RS): K1, p1, *k3, p1; rep from * to last 2 sts, k2.

Rep the rows 1 and 2 once more.

Next row (WS): P1, m1, knit to last st, m1, p1—
34 (38, 38, 42) sts.

Sleeve Shaping

Continuing in waffle stitch as established, inc after first
st and before last st every 5th row 17 (17, 18, 18) times—
68 (72, 74, 78) sts.

Continue in waffle stitch without further shaping until
sleeve measures 19 (19½, 20, 20) inches.

BO in patt.

Make second sleeve same as the first.

Finishing

Weave in loose ends. Block pieces, if desired, and if
your yarn's care instructions allow, using the instructions on pages 60–62.

Fold sleeves in half lengthwise, with RS facing each
other, and sew underarm seam using backstitch (see
page 65).

Pin front shoulders to back shoulders with WS facing
each other and use backstitch to sew shoulder seams
on RS. (This is called reverse seaming and gives you a
raised seam on the RS.)

Pin sleeves into armholes, WS facing each other, easing
where necessary, and reverse-seam sleeves to armhole
as for shoulder seams.

Sew bottom of buttonhole band to corresponding
stitches on right front.

Join CC with a slipstitch to bottom edge of button band
and work single crochet (see page 80) up side of buttonhole band and across top of buttonhole band.

Sew buttons to right front button band to correspond
with buttonholes.

Block again, if desired, and if your yarn's care instructions allow, using the instructions on pages 60–62.

Marly Mittens

Skill Level – Easy    *Designer – Sharon Turner*

These extra warm mittens will keep your hands toasty on chilly days, and you won't lose them because they have a handy mitten chain holding them together. (Little kids are the only ones who think mitten chains are uncool.)

These mitts knit up extra quick—3 hours tops—in a double strand of chunky yarn (only 2 stitches per inch!). Plus, you knit both the right and left mitten the same way—except in different color combinations—so you don't have to worry about getting all mixed up with lefts and rights.

specifications

Size

S (L)

Size shown: S

Finished Measurements

Hand circumference: 8 (10) inches

Materials

- 1 ball GGH/Muench *Via Mala* (100% wool, 73 yd./50 g ball) color #20 (A), 1 ball color #42 (B), and 1 ball color #31 (C)
- US 17 (12 mm) double-pointed needles, set of 4
- Split-ring stitch marker
- Small stitch holder or safety pin
- Tapestry needle

Gauge

8 sts and 12 rows to 4 inches in stockinette stitch *using yarn held double* on US 17 (12 mm) needles, or size needed to obtain gauge

note: If you decide to use different yarn to make this pattern, look for yarn that by itself has a gauge of 12 sts to 4 inches in stockinette stitch on US 10 (6 mm) needles.

Pattern Stitches

St st (Stockinette stitch) Worked in Rnds

Knit every rnd.

k2tog (knit 2 together)

Insert the right needle into the front of the next 2 sts on the left needle as if to knit. Wrap the yarn over the right needle and knit the 2 sts as 1 st.

instructions

Right Mitten

With A and B held tog, use the long–tail cast–on method (see page 13) to CO 16 (20) sts to a dpn. Divide sts as evenly as possible over 3 dpns. Place marker on first st to note beginning of rnd and join sts in a circle, being careful not to twist sts.

Knit every round until mitten measures 3 inches from beg.

Next rnd—work thumbhole: K1, place next 3 sts on holder or safety pin; CO 3 sts to the right (working) needle, using backward-loop method (see page 13), and knit to end of rnd.

Knit every rnd until mitten measures 7 (8) inches (or until mitten reaches the tip of the pinky).

Mitten Tip Shaping

Next rnd: *K2, k2tog; rep from * to end—12 (15) sts.

Next rnd: Knit.

Next rnd: *K2tog; rep from * 5 (6) times, end k0 (1)—6 (8) sts.

Cut yarn, leaving a 10-inch tail. Pull through rem 6 (8) sts, and tighten.

Thumb

Join yarn (same two yarns as for mitten body) and use a dpn to knit across the 3 thumb sts from the holder. Using a second dpn, pick up and k1 st at left side of thumb opening, then pick up and k3 sts from the top of the thumb opening. Use a third dpn to pick up and k1 st from right side of thumb opening—8 sts.

note: For a refresher on picking up stitches, see pages 68–69.

Rearrange the sts so that the last 2 sts are on the third dpn.

Place marker and join rnd, being careful not to twist sts. Knit every rnd until thumb measures approx 1¾ (2) inches or to midpoint of the thumbnail.

Thumb Tip Shaping

Next rnd: *K2, k2tog; rep from * to end—6 sts.

Next rnd: Knit.

Cut yarn, leaving an 8-inch tail. Thread tail into a tapestry needle, pull through rem 6 sts, and tighten.

Left Mitten

Work as for right mitten, using A and C held together.

Mitten Chain

Cut one strand each B and C about 150–160 inches long. Knot the strands together at each end. Loop one knotted end to a wall hook or have someone hold it for you. Hold the other knotted end yourself and twist it until the strands are tightly spun together. Maintaining tight tension on the strands, and taking care not to let them untwist, fold the strands in half—holding the fold loop firmly in one hand—so that the knotted ends are lined up with each other. Let go of the fold loop; the cord twists itself together, forming a mitten chain.

Finishing

Weave in ends, stitching up any holes around base of thumb, if necessary.

Lightly steam to block, if desired, and if your yarn's care instructions allow, using the instructions on page 61.

Sew mitten chain ends to inside corners of mitten cuffs.

Phone/MP3 Player Sweater

Skill Level – Easy  *Designer – Sharon Turner*

Here's a quick and easy project that you can knit to dress up your mobile phone or MP3 player. You can use up scrap yarn for this project, or if you buy the yarn to make the little sweater, you'll have enough to make several as gifts for your friends.

specifications

Size

One size

Finished Measurements

Height: 3½ inches

Width: 3¼ inches

Materials

- 1 ball elann.com *Super Cable Aran* (100% mercerized cotton, 93 yd./50 g ball) color #0143 (A), 1 ball color #2503 (B), and 1 ball color #0076 (C)
- US 7 (4.5 mm) needles
- US 7 (4.5 mm) double–pointed needles, for working handle
- Tapestry needle
- 3 ⅜-inch buttons to match C
- Sewing needle

Gauge

18 sts and 27 rows to 4 inches in stockinette stitch on US 7 (4.5 mm) needles, or size needed to obtain gauge

Pattern Stitches

St st (Stockinette Stitch) Worked in Rows

Row 1 (RS): Knit.

Row 2 (WS): Purl.

Rep rows 1 and 2 for St st worked in rows.

Stripe Pattern (Worked in Stockinette Stitch)

2 rows A

2 rows B

m1 (Make 1)

Increase 1 st by using the left needle to pick up the horizontal strand from front to back between the last st worked on the right needle and the next st to be worked on the left needle and knit into the picked–up strand.

instructions

Body

With straight needles and A, use the long–tail CO method (see page 13) to CO 15 sts.

Work in St st and stripe patt for approx 7–7½ inches or to suit double the length of phone or MP3 player, ending with a WS row in A. Still using A, BO knitwise.

Sleeves

With straight needles and A, use the long–tail CO method (see page 13) to CO 6 sts. Work in St st and stripe patt for 4 rows.

Maintaining stripe patt, inc 1 st using m1 at each end of next row and then every following 4th row 3 times—14 sts.

Finish 2nd row of 9th stripe. Still using A, BO knitwise.

Make 2nd sleeve same as the first.

Handle

With dpns and C, use the long–tail CO method (see page 13) to CO 4 sts, leaving an 8–inch tail.

Work knitted cord (see page 59) for 4½ inches.

Cut yarn, leaving an 8–inch tail. Pull tail through sts and tighten.

Finishing

Weave in ends, except for the tails left from casting on and binding off. Fold sleeves in half lengthwise with WS facing each other and use tail to whipstitch (see page 76) underarm seam. Fold body in half, holding cast–on edge to bound–off edge, with WS facing each other, and use mattress stitch to sew side seams from top edge down to fold. The sleeves are not functional, so you can just whipstitch the sleeve caps to top of body sides.

Lightly steam, if necessary, and if your yarn's care instructions allow.

Use tails to sew the handle ends to the top corners of the sweater. Sew buttons down the front.

Chapter 12

dancer

What's the connection between knitting and dancing? Is it the need to be always in motion, or is it liking to count beats, steps, and stitches? Whatever it is, a lot of dancers are knitters, too. The projects in this section are designed with dancers in mind, but even if you're not into dance, you'll probably like the ballet shrug, the cute little wrap skirt, the leg warmers, and the fun felted floral hair ornament.

If you're looking for a nice carryall to suit your active style, turn to page 115 for the big Flower Power Purse. It's roomy enough to tote your dance stuff, and you can tuck in your knitting right next to the ballet slippers. So take off your tap shoes, grab your knitting needles, and get clicking!

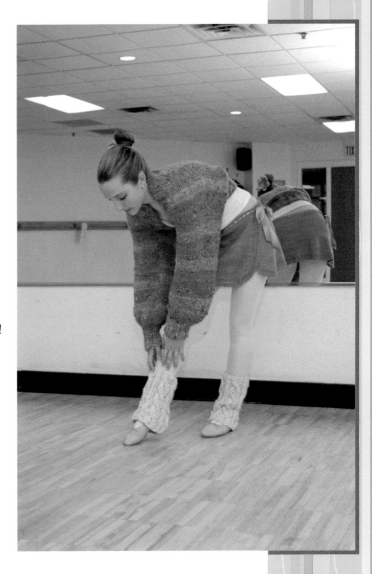

Ballet Shrug

Skill Level – Easy   *Designer – Sharon Turner*

This shrug will keep you warm on the way to dance class or during breaks at practice. Or, if you're not a dancer, wear it with a tight-fitting tee and jeans. It's a cinch to make: knit cuff to cuff with no shaping, it's just a big rectangle. No need to sacrifice fashion if you're a knitting beginner! The ribbing around the waist, front, and neck is worked in the round by picking up stitches around the opening that forms after the sleeve seams are sewn. The subtle self-striping effect created by this fun yarn takes the monotony out of knitting such a big piece, too.

specifications

Size

XS (S, M, L)

Size shown: S

Finished Measurements

Cuff-to-cuff width: 64 (67, 71, 74) inches

Waist-to-neck length: 14½ (17¼, 20, 22½) inches, not including ribbing

Materials

- 7 (7, 8, 9) balls GGH/Muench *Alexis* (60% wool/40% nylon, 87 yd./50 g ball) color #003 (A)

- 4 (4, 5, 6) balls GGH/Muench *Soft Kid* (70% kid mohair, 25% nylon, 5% wool, 150 yd./25 g ball) color #073 (B)

note: The shrug is knit using one strand each A and B at the same time.

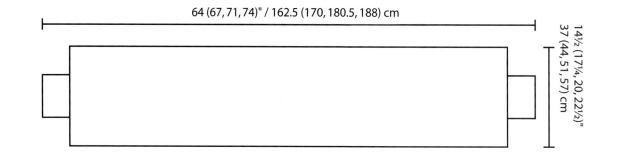

64 (67, 71, 74)" / 162.5 (170, 180.5, 188) cm

14½ (17¼, 20, 22½)"
37 (44, 51, 57) cm

- US 11 (8 mm) 29- to 36-inch circular needle

- Stitch marker

- Tapestry needle

Gauge

12 sts and 16 rows to 4 inches in stockinette stitch on US 11 (8 mm) needles *using yarns A and B held together*, or size needed to obtain gauge

Pattern Stitches

2 x 2 Rib (Mult of 4 Sts Plus 2) Worked in Rows

Row 1 (RS): K2, *p2, k2; rep from * to end.

Row 2 (WS): P2, *k2, p2; rep from * to end.

Rep rows 1 and 2 for 2 x 2 rib worked in rows.

2 x 2 Rib (Mult of 4 Sts) Worked in Rnds

Rnd 1: *K2, p2; rep from * to end of rnd.

Rep rnd 1 for 2 x 2 rib worked in rnds.

kfb (knit into front and back)

Increase 1 st by knitting into the front and then into the back of the next st.

St st (stockinette stitch) Worked in Rows

Row 1 (RS): Knit.

Row 2 (WS): Purl.

Rep rnds 1 and 2 for St st worked in rows.

k2tog (Knit 2 Together)

Insert the right needle into the front of the next 2 sts on the left needle as if to knit. Wrap the yarn over the right needle and knit the 2 sts as 1 st.

instructions

note: The body of the shrug is knit flat from cuff to cuff. The width from cuff to cuff is generous, to allow for the puffiness above the cuff. After you sew the sleeve seams, you work the ribbing around the waist, fronts, and neck in the round as one piece.

Ribbed Cuff

Holding one strand each A and B together, use the long-tail cast-on method (see page 13) to CO 22 (26, 30, 34) sts. Work 2 x 2 rib as follows:

> **Row 1 (RS):** K2, *p2, k2; rep from * to end.
>
> **Row 2 (WS):** P2, *k2, p2; rep from * to end.

Rep rows 1 and 2 until cuff measures 4 (4, 5, 5) inches from CO edge, ending with a WS row.

Cuff

Next row—dec row (RS): *K2tog; rep from * to end—22 (26, 30, 34) sts.

Beg with a WS row (row 2 of rib instructions), work 2 x 2 rib as follows:

Row 1 (RS): K2, *p2, k2; rep from * to end.

Row 2 (WS): P2, *k2, p2; rep from * to end.

Rep rows 1 and 2 until cuff measures 4 (4, 5, 5) inches. BO in patt.

Finishing

Weave in ends. Steam piece to block (see page 61), avoiding the ribbed cuffs.

Beg at one of the cuffs, use mattress stitch (see page 63) to sew sleeve seam for 19 (19¾, 20¼, 21) inches. Rep for other sleeve seam. You should have an opening in the middle.

Steam seams to neaten.

Ribbed Waistband/Neckband

note: For a refresher on picking up stitches, see pages 68–69.

With RS facing and beg at the end of one of the sleeve seams, pick up and k70 (74, 82, 86) sts evenly across one side of the opening to the other sleeve seam end; pick up and k70 (74, 82, 86) sts evenly across the other side of the opening back to where you began—140 (148, 164, 172) sts. Place marker to note end of rnd and join rnd, being careful not to twist sts.

Work in 2 x 2 rib as follows:

Rnd 1: *K2, p2; rep from * to end of rnd.

Rep rnd 1 until ribbing measures 2½–3 inches from beg. BO in patt.

Weave in ends.

Body

Next row—inc row (RS): *Kfb; rep from * to end—44 (52, 60, 68) sts.

Beg with a purl row, work in St st until piece measures 60 (63, 66, 69) inches from CO edge, ending with a WS row.

Pirouette

Skill Level – Easy/Intermediate   *Designer – Claudine Monique*

Here's a flirty ballet wrap skirt with lace trim to wear over your leotard during dance class. After class, slip on a pair of leggings underneath for hanging out with your friends.

specifications

Size

S (M, L)

Size shown: S

Finished Measurements

Waist (unwrapped): 30 (35¼, 40¾) inches

Hip (unwrapped): 43½ (49, 54½) inches

Length (including trim): 11 (12, 13) inches

Materials

- 3 (4, 5) balls Artyarns *Ultramerino 4* (100% merino wool, 191 yd./50 g ball) color #247
- US 4 (3.5 mm) 24– to 29–inch circular needle
- US 2 (2.75) needles
- Stitch markers
- Tapestry needle
- 1½ yd. 1-inch satin ribbon
- 2 small snaps
- Sewing needle and thread that matches yarn

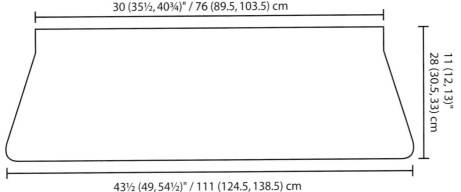

30 (35½, 40¾)" / 76 (89.5, 103.5) cm

11 (12, 13)" / 28 (30.5, 33) cm

43½ (49, 54½)" / 111 (124.5, 138.5) cm

Gauge

22 sts and 30 rows to 4 inches in reverse stockinette stitch on US 4 (3.5 mm) needles, or size needed to obtain gauge

Pattern Stitches

rev St st (Reverse Stockinette Stitch) Worked in Rows

Row 1 (RS): Purl.

Row 2 (WS): Knit.

Rep rows 1 and 2 for rev St st worked in rows.

Garter Stitch Worked in Rows

Knit all rows.

p2tog (Purl 2 Together)

Insert the right needle into the front of the next 2 sts on the left needle as if to purl. Wrap the yarn over the right needle and purl the 2 sts as 1 st.

yo (Yarn Over)

Bring the working yarn to the front of the needles and lay it over the right needle from front to back. This cre-ates another stitch.

k2tog (Knit 2 Together)

Insert the right needle into the front of the next 2 sts on the left needle as if to knit. Wrap the yarn over the right needle and knit the 2 sts as 1 st.

Lace Edging (7 Sts)

Row 1: K3, yo, k2tog, yo twice, k2—9 sts.

Row 2: K2, knit into the front and then back of dou-ble yo, k2, yo, k2tog, k1—9 sts.

Row 3: K3, yo, k2tog, k4—9 sts.

Row 4: BO 2 sts, k3, yo, k2tog, k1—7 sts.

Rep rows 1–4 for lace edging.

instructions

Skirt Body

Using circular needle and long-tail cast-on method (see page 13), CO 240 (270, 300) sts.

Row 1 (RS): Purl.

Row 2 (WS): Knit.

Short Rows

note: For a refresher on short-row shaping, see page 35.

The rounded edges at the front edges of the skirt are formed using short-row shaping as follows:

Row 1 (RS): Purl to the last 3 sts, bring yarn to back of work, slip next st to right needle, bring yarn to front of work, slip st back to left needle. (This is your first "wrapped" st.)

Row 2 (WS): Turn to the WS and knit to the last 3 sts, bring yarn to front of work, slip next st to right needle, bring yarn to back of work, and slip st back to left needle.

Row 3: Turn and purl until 1 st before wrapped st, bring yarn to back of work, slip next st, bring yarn to front of work.

Continue in rev St st as established, wrapping each st before the last one wrapped, until 12 sts remain at each end of row.

Next row (RS): Purl to first wrapped st. Pick up wrap from underneath (inserting needle from back to front) with right needle, place wrap on left needle, purl together the st and the wrap. Rep to end of row.

Next row (WS): Knit to the first wrapped st, slip st to right needle, pick up wrap with left needle, slip st back to left needle, knit together the st and wrap. Rep, knitting sts and their corresponding wraps tog, to end of row.

Top of Skirt

Work without further shaping until piece measures 3 (4, 5) inches from CO edge, ending with a WS row.

Place markers 69 (77, 85) sts from each end, leaving 102 (116, 130) sts between the markers.

note: These markers represent where your "side seams" would be.

Next row (RS): Purl to 3 sts before first marker, p2tog, p1, slip marker, p1, p2tog, purl to 3 sts before next marker, p2tog, p1, slip marker, p1, p2tog, purl to end of row—236 (266, 296) sts.

Work 3 rows in rev St st without shaping.

Rep last 4 rows 13 times—184 (214, 244) sts.

Continue without further shaping until piece measures 9 (10, 11) inches from CO edge (measuring mid-row, not from rounded front edges), ending with a WS row.

Waistband

note: Except for the row after the eyelet row, the waistband is worked entirely in garter stitch.

Next row (RS): K6 (10, 8), k2tog, *k7 (8, 10), k2tog; rep from * to last 5 (12, 6) sts, k5 (12, 6) —164 (194, 224) sts.

Knit 3 rows without shaping.

Next row—work eyelets (RS): K1, *k2tog, yo; rep from * to last st, k1.
Next row (WS): Purl.

Knit 4 rows. BO all sts.

Lace Edging

Using smaller needles, CO 7 sts. Knit 5 rows.

Begin working lace edging as follows:

Row 1: K3, yo, k2tog, yo twice, k2—9 sts.
Row 2: K2, knit into the front and then back of double yo, k2, yo, k2tog, k1—9 sts.
Row 3: K3, yo, k2tog, k4—9 sts.
Row 4: BO 2 sts, k3, yo, k2tog, k1—7 sts.

Rep rows 1–4 until lace fits all around front and hem edges, minus ½ inch, ending with row 4 of patt.

Knit 5 rows.

BO all sts.

Finishing

Block, if desired, and if yarn manufacturer's care instructions allow, using the instructions on pages 60–62.

Whipstitch (see page 76) lace border to front edges and hem of skirt.

Weave in ends.

With sewing needle and thread, sew snaps onto fronts of skirt on inside, adjusting placement to fit your waist.

Place skirt right side up, with snaps fastened. Thread ribbon though eyelets on waistband of skirt, starting and ending at front edge. Leave long tail of ribbon on both ends.

Ankle Warmers

Skill Level – Easy   *Designer – Sharon Turner*

You don't have to be a dancer to appreciate a good pair of leg warmers. Easy and quick to make, these short leg warmers—ankle warmers, actually— are worked in a no-brainer cable pattern on big needles, holding the two luxurious angora and alpaca-blend yarns together. If you decide to make them longer, just remember to buy an extra ball of yarn.

specifications

Size

S (M, L)

Size shown: M

Finished Measurements

Length: 9½ inches

Circumference: 8 (10½, 13½) inches

Materials

- 2 hanks Cascade Yarns *Dolce* (55% alpaca/23% wool/22% silk, 109 yd./50 g ball) color #938 (A)

- 2 balls Cascade Yarns *Cloud 9* (50% merino/50% angora, 109 yd./50 g ball) in color #101 (B)

note: The ankle warmers are knit using one strand each A and B held together.

- US 11 (8 mm) double-pointed needles, set of 4
- US 13 (9 mm) double-pointed needles, set of 4
- Cable needle
- Row counter (optional)
- Split-ring stitch marker
- Tapestry needle

Gauge

18 sts and 15 rnds to 4 inches in cable rib pattern on US 13 (9 mm) needles *using yarns A and B held together*, or size needed to obtain gauge

note: If you decide to use different yarn to make this pattern, look for yarn that by itself has a gauge of 20–22 sts to 4 inches in stockinette stitch on US 6–7 (4–4.5 mm) needles.

Pattern Stitches

2 x 2 Rib (Mult of 4 Sts) Worked in Rnds

Rnd 1: *K2, p2; rep from * to end.

Rep rnd 1 for 2 x 2 rib worked in rnds.

Cable Rib (Mult of 12 sts) Worked in Rnds

Rnds 1 and 2: *K2, p2; rep from * to end.

Rnd 3: *K2, p2, slip next 3 sts to cable needle and hold to front, k2, p1 from left needle, k3 from cable needle, p2; rep from * to end.

Rnds 4–8: *K2, p2; rep from * to end.

Rep rnds 1–8 for cable rib worked in rnds.

instructions

Holding one strand each of A and B together and using the long–tail cast–on method (see page 13), CO 36 (48, 60) sts to one of the smaller dpns. Divide sts evenly over 3 dpns. Place marker on first st to note beginning of rnd and join rnd, being careful not to twist sts.

Ribbing

Work 3 rnds in 2 x 2 rib.

Cable Rib Patt

Change to larger dpns and, beg with rnd 1, work in cable rib patt for 29 rnds. (If necessary, use a row counter to keep track of rows.) Change to smaller dpns and work 3 more rnds.

BO in 2 x 2 rib.

Finishing

Weave in ends.

Floral Hair Ornament

Skill Level – Easy   **Designer – Claudine Monique**

Every ballerina needs a little extra something every now and then. This *ornement floral* is the perfect accessory to complete your outfit. It is not only perfect for ballet class but for everyday use. Make one in every color of the rainbow. These also make great last-minute gifts for friends.

If you decide to substitute a different yarn in this pattern, keep in mind that only animal fibers felt, so you must use a yarn that is at least 85% wool, alpaca, or another animal fiber.

specifications

Size
One size

Finished Measurements (After Felting)
Diameter: Approximately 4 inches

Materials
- 1 ball elann.com *Highland Wool* (100% wool, 109 yd./50 g ball) color #2507 (A) and 1 ball color #5420 (B)

hint: Each skein makes about 3 flowers. Use your leftover yarn to make some for your ballet classmates.

- US 10 (6 mm) double–pointed needles, set of 5
- Split–ring stitch marker
- Tapestry needle
- Sewing needle and thread that matches yarn
- Elastic hair band
- A variety of small buttons
- Zippered pillowcase or lingerie bag (for felting)

Gauge (Before Felting)
14 sts and 17 rows to 4 inches in stockinette stitch on US 10 (6 mm) needles, or size needed to obtain gauge

Pattern Stitches
St st (Stockinette Stitch) Worked in Rows
Row 1 (RS): Knit.

Row 2 (WS): Purl.

Rep rows 1 and 2 for St st worked in rows.

kfb (Knit into Front and Back)
Increase 1 st by knitting into the front and then into the back of the next st.

k2tog (Knit 2 Together)
Insert the right needle into the front of the next 2 sts on the left needle as if to knit. Wrap the yarn over the right needle and knit the 2 sts as 1 st.

instructions
Make one flower, as follows, in each color.

Make Petal

note: For this part of the flower, you need only 2 dpns.

CO 4 sts to a dpn.

Row 1 and all other WS rows: Purl.

Row 2 (RS): Kfb, k2, kfb—6 sts.

Row 4: Kfb, k4, kfb—8 sts.

Row 6: Kfb, k6, kfb—10 sts.

Row 8: Knit.

Row 10: K2tog, k6, k2tog—8 sts.

Row 12: K2tog, k4, k2tog—6 sts.

Cut yarn, leaving a 6-inch tail, and put sts on a spare needle.

Rep 5 times more to create 6 petals. On the last petal, do not cut yarn.

Join Petals

Spread petal sts evenly over 3 or 4 dpns, making sure the petal with the working yarn attached is positioned to join the rnd—36 sts.

Place marker to note beginning of rnd and join rnd, being careful not to twist sts.

Rnd 1 and all other odd-numbered rnds: Knit.

Rnd 2: *K2tog, k2, k2tog; rep from * to end—24 sts.

Rnd 4: *K2tog; rep from * to end—12 sts.

Rnd 6: *K2tog; rep from * to end—6 sts.

Cut yarn, leaving a 6-inch tail, draw though remaining sts, and tighten.

Finishing

Weave in all ends.

Felting

To felt your flowers, put them in a zippered pillowcase or lingerie bag. Set the washer for a small load at the hottest setting and fill, adding a tablespoon of mild laundry or dish detergent. When the washer is done filling, put in the zippered pillowcase and a pair of jeans or an old canvas sneaker for added friction. Periodically check on the felting during the wash cycle, but stop it before it progresses to the rinse cycle. Rep if necessary, until the flowers are felted to your preference and to the desired size.

Take the flowers out of the washing machine and rinse them by hand. Return the pieces to the washing machine and spin the excess water out of them. Remove from the washer and lay them flat to dry. If you would like your flowers to have a funky look, pull on the petals to shape them before they dry. (You can always wet the petals and reshape them if you don't like your first attempt.)

Assembly

With sewing needle and thread, sew a variety of buttons onto the center of the flower you want to be on top.

Sew the other flower to the bottom of the first, twisting the bottom flower so that it shows between the petals of the top flower. Using a double strand of thread, attach the flower to an elastic hair band.

Chapter 13
girly-girl

Admit it, you're a girly-girl. You like pink; you like ruffles, you like flowers. You adore accessorizing, and you have a closet full of clothes, shoes, bags, scarves, and lots of jewelry. Why? Because that kind of stuff is fun! Whether you're dressing up for a party or just heading off to hang out with friends, you must primp—at least a little—and put on some earrings and a bracelet or two. And spend at least 10 minutes on your hair.

Now that you're a *knitting* girly-girl, you can knit yourself all kinds of accessories, sweaters, and bags. This chapter gives you some girly, fun-to-knit patterns: two beautiful felted bags—large and small—to cover all your toting needs, a ruffled wrap, and a fancy headband. (You'll also like the shrug and hair ornament in Chapter 12, not to mention the ruffled skirt, clutch, and mini stole in Chapter 14—so be sure to check those out, too.)

Flower Power Purses

Skill Level – Intermediate   *Designer – Alison Stewart-Guinee*

These happy bags are just the thing for the girl on the go. Designed to carry everything but the kitchen sink, the larger bag is roomy enough to go from school to sleepover, while its smaller twin is just perfect for shopping trips or a night on the town. So that no girl has to sacrifice fashion for function ever again, each bag is adorned with a knitted and felted flower. Both bags are knit using the same pattern, from the bottom up, and then felted into a dense fabric, making them ever so sturdy and dependable.

If you decide to substitute a different yarn in this pattern, keep in mind that only animal fibers felt, so you must use a yarn that is at least 85% wool, alpaca, or another animal fiber.

specifications

Size

S (L)

Sizes shown: S (L)

Finished Measurements (After Felting)

Height: 7 (14) inches (including ruffle)

Width: 8 (17) inches

Base: 6½ x 3 inches (14½ x 5¼ inches)

note: The finished size of your bag may vary, depending on the degree of felting. The finished measurements of these bags reflect a densely felted fabric.

Materials

- 2 (5) skeins Cascade Yarns *Cascade 220* (100% wool, 220 yd./100 g skein) color #9438 (A), 2 (5) skeins color #7802 (B), 1 skein color #9461 (C), and 1 (3) skeins color #7919 (D)

- US 10½ (6.5 mm) 16–inch circular needle for small bag

- US 11 (8 mm) 24–inch circular needle for small bag

- US 10½ (6.5 mm) 24–inch circular needle for large bag
- US 11 (8 mm) 32–inch circular needle for large bag
- Stitch markers
- Tapestry needle
- Upholstery thread that matches yarn
- Sewing needle
- Several beads or buttons for embellishing flower
- Purchased handles for small bag
- ½ yd. ribbon for attaching the purchased handles to the small bag
- Cardboard or foam core for bag base (optional)
- Fabric for covering bag base (optional)
- Zippered pillowcase or lingerie bag (for felting)

Gauge (Before Felting)

11 sts and 20 rows to 4 inches *using yarn held double* in garter stitch on US 11 (8 mm) needles, or size needed to obtain gauge

note: If you decide to use different yarn to make this pattern, look for yarn that by itself has a gauge of 18–20 sts to 4 inches in stockinette stitch on US 7–8 (4.5–5 mm) needles.

Pattern Stitches

Garter Stitch Worked in Rows

Knit all rows.

kfb (Knit into Front and Back)

Increase 1 st by knitting into the front and then into the back of the next st.

k2tog (Knit 2 Together)

Insert the right needle into the front of the next 2 sts on the left needle as if to knit. Wrap the yarn over the right needle and knit the 2 sts as 1 st.

m1 (Make 1)

Increase 1 st by using the left needle to pick up the horizontal strand from front to back between the last st worked on the right needle and the next st to be worked on the left needle and knit into the picked–up strand.

ssk (Slip, Slip, Knit)

Insert the right needle from front to back into the front of the next st on the left needle and slip it onto the right needle. Repeat this with the next st. (You have slipped 2 sts knitwise from the left needle to the right needle.) Insert the left needle into the fronts of both slipped sts and then knit them as 1 st.

p2tog (Purl 2 Together)

Insert the right needle into the front of the next 2 sts on the left needle as if to purl. Wrap the yarn over the right needle and purl the 2 sts as 1 st.

p2tog tbl (Purl 2 Together Through Back Loops)

Insert the right needle into the back of the next 2 sts on the left needle as if to purl. Wrap the yarn over the right needle and purl the 2 sts as 1 st.

yo (Yarn Over)

Bring the working yarn to the front of the needles and lay it over the right needle from front to back. This creates another stitch.

psso (pass slipped stitch over)

Pass the slipped st over the last st(s) worked.

instructions

note: The yarn is held double throughout this project.

Bag Base

Using two strands of A and larger needle, use the long–tail cast-on method (see page 13) to CO 22 (55) sts. Working back and forth in rows, work 15 (31) rows in garter stitch.

Do not turn work after the last row. This is the right side of the piece and will form the bottom of the bag. The remainder of the bag will be worked in rnds.

With smaller needle, place marker and pick up and k11 (22) sts along the short end of the piece adjacent to the corner where the last st was knitted. Place second marker, rotate the work, and pick up and k22 (55) sts along the long side of the piece. Place third marker, rotate the work, and pick up and k11 (22) sts along the remaining short side of the piece—66 (154) sts total,

including the original 22 (55) sts. Place a fourth, contrasting, marker at this corner.

note: The contrasting marker signifies the beginning of the rnd. The remaining three markers help you keep track of the pattern. Each of the four sides ends with a full pattern repeat. All markers need to be slipped as the work progresses.

Using larger needle, purl 3 rnds. These rnds form the turning ridge of the bag base. Cut A, leaving a 6-inch tail.

Bag Body

Join a double strand of B and work pattern setup rnds as follows:

> **Rnds 1, 3, and 5:** Knit.
>
> **Rnds 2, 4, and 6:** Purl.

Cut B, leaving a 6-inch tail.

Wave Pattern

> **Rnd 1:** Join a double strand of A and *k2tog, k2, kfb twice, k3, ssk; rep from * to end.
>
> **Rnds 2–6:** Knit.

Cut A, leaving a 6-inch tail.

> **Rnd 7:** Join a double strand of B and *k2tog, k2, kfb twice, k3, ssk; rep from * to end.
>
> **Rnds 8, 10, and 12:** Purl.
>
> **Rnds 9 and 11:** Knit.

Cut B, leaving a 6-inch tail.

Rep rnds 1–12 1 (6) times—24 (84) rnds total worked in wave pattern.

Join a double strand of C and change to smaller needle.

> **Next rnd:** Knit.
>
> **Next rnd:** Purl.

A total of 32 (92) rnds have been worked after turning ridge.

Ruffle

Join a double strand of D and switch to larger needle.

> **Rnds 1 and 3:** Knit.
>
> **Rnd 2:** *Kfb; rep from * to end—132 (308) sts.

Rnd 4: *Kfb; rep from * to end—264 (616) sts.

Rnds 5–7: Knit.

For the small bag, BO all sts.

For the large bag, knit 2 rnds and then BO all sts.

Handles for Large Bag (Make 2)

With double strand of B and using larger needle, use the long-tail cast-on method (see page 13) to CO 130 sts. Work handles back and forth in rows as follows:

Row 1 (RS): K43, place marker, k44, place marker, k43.

Row 2 (WS): K43, p44, k43.

Row 3: Knit.

Repeat last 2 rows 5 times more—13 rows completed.

BO knitwise.

Close the center section of each handle by whipstitching a seam (see page 76) along the 44 middle sts, with RS together. Turn handle right-side out.

Flower
Flower Base

With a double strand of D and using the larger needle, CO 3 sts.

Row 1 (RS): Sl 1, m1, knit to end—4 sts.

note: The abbreviation *sl 1* means slip 1 stitch. (For a refresher on slipping stitches, see page 33.)

Row 2 (WS): Sl 1, m1, purl to end—5 sts.

Rep these 2 rows 4 times more—13 sts.

Next row (RS): Knit.

Next row (WS): Purl.

Rep these 2 rows 2 times more.

Next row: (Ssk) 3 times, k1, (k2tog) 3 times—7 sts.

Next row: Sl 1, p2tog, p1, p2tog tbl, p1—5 sts.

Cut yarn and keep live sts on the needle so you can join the flower together later.

With RS facing and using the same needle, repeat this process 4 times more, for a total of 5 petals. Do not cut yarn after knitting the fifth petal.

With RS of petals facing, knit across all 5 petals, using the working yarn trailing from the fifth petal to join them together—25 sts.

Cut yarn, leaving a generous tail. Thread the tail onto a tapestry needle and snugly gather the sts into a rnd by running the tapestry needle through the live sts on the needle.

Sepals

Using a double strand of B and larger needle, make a slipknot on the needle in your left hand. Using the backward-loop CO method (see page 13), *CO 5 sts, then BO these 5 sts. At this point, all the sts are off the left needle, and there is 1 st remaining on the right needle. Slip the st on the right needle back to the left needle and rep from * 4 times. After the fifth sepal, fasten off and cut the yarn, leaving enough yarn to gather the sts together in a rnd as you did for the flower base. Because there are no live sts to run the end through, you run the tail through the sts at the base of each sepal.

Repeat this process to make the larger sepal piece by using a double strand of A and casting on and binding off 9 sts instead of 5.

Leaves

Make one leaf for the small bag and two leaves for the large bag, as follows:

With double strand of C and larger needle, CO 5 sts.

Row 1 (RS): K2, yo, k1, yo, k2—7 sts.
Row 2 and all other WS rows: Purl.
Row 3: K3, yo, k1, yo, k3—9 sts.
Row 5: K4, yo, k1, yo, k4—11 sts.
Row 7: Ssk, k7, k2tog—9 sts.
Row 9: Ssk, k5, k2tog—7 sts.
Row 11: Ssk, k3, k2tog—5 sts.
Row 13: Ssk, k1, k2tog—3 sts.
Row 15: Sl 1, k2tog, psso—1 st.

Cut yarn, pull through last st, and secure.

Finishing

Weave in ends.

Felting

Place the individual knitted pieces inside a zippered pillowcase or lingerie bag. Felt the pieces in a washing machine with hot water and a small amount of detergent. Adding a pair of jeans or similar garment to the washer helps facilitate the felting process by creating more friction. Allow the washer to complete the wash and agitation cycle, but stop it before it progresses to the rinse cycle. Check your knitted items, and if they're not yet felted enough, turn the washer setting back to the agitation portion of the wash cycle. Repeat as many times as desired. The more times the pieces go through the agitation portion of the wash cycle, the more they will felt. The number of agitation cycles needed varies from washer to washer.

If the water begins to cool during felting, add more hot water. When the pieces have felted to the desired degree, take them out of the machine and rinse them by hand. Return the pieces to the washing machine and spin the excess water out of them. Remove from washer.

Blocking

Pull the bag, handles, flowers, and leaves into the shape desired, making sure that the size of the bag is even all around. Put a piece of cardboard in the bottom of the bag to give structure to its base. Fill the bag with paper or plastic bags to shape as desired and let the pieces air dry. Do not begin assembly until the flower pieces, handles, and bag are completely dry.

Assembly

Layer the pieces of the flower together as shown and use a sewing needle to sew them to one another with upholstery thread. Embellish the center of the flower with beads or a button, as desired. Sew the flower to the body of the bag. Position leaf or leaves around flower and sew in place.

Sew the knitted handles to the large bag.

To attach the purchased handles to the smaller bag, cut a 3- to 4-inch piece of ribbon for each handle opening. Fold the ribbon into a loop, as shown, and sew each loop around the handle opening. Attach the handles to the bag by sewing the ribbon loops to the bags.

Bag Base (Optional)

If you want to give structure to the base of the bag, cut a piece of cardboard or foam core the same size as your bag's base. If desired, cover the cardboard or foam core by cutting two pieces of fabric large enough to cover the board, plus a ½–inch seam allowance for each edge. With right sides of the fabric together, sew along three sides, leaving the fourth side open. Turn right–side out. Slip the cardboard or foam core into the fabric sleeve, fold the opening at the fourth side to the inside, and stitch closed. Place base in the bottom of the bag.

Pretty in Pink

Skill Level – Intermediate  **Designer – Alison Stewart-Guinee**

Light as a feather and silky soft, this little wrap is a dream come true. Knit out of a lace-weight mohair/silk blend, it will keep you warm on the coldest winter days without weighing you down. The ruching in this design is easily achieved with a switch of needle size and simple increases and decreases, making knitting a breeze.

specifications

Size

One size

Finished Measurements

Width: 10 inches

Length: 60 inches

Materials

- 2 skeins Cascade Yarns *Kid Seta* (70% super kid mohair/30% silk, 230 yd./25 g skein) color #830 (MC) and 1 skein color #460 (CC)
- US 7 (4.5 mm) needles
- US 6 (4 mm) needles
- Tapestry needle

Gauge

21 sts and 28 rows to 4 inches in stockinette stitch on US 7 (4.5 mm) needles, or size needed to obtain gauge

Pattern Stitches

kfb (Knit into Front and Back)

Increase 1 st by knitting into the front and then into the back of the next st.

kfb&f (Knit into Front, Back, and Front)

Increase 2 sts by knitting into the front, back, and front again of the next st.

St st (Stockinette Stitch) Worked in Rows

Row 1 (RS): Knit.

Row 2 (WS): Purl.

Rep rows 1 and 2 for St st worked in rows.

instructions

Ruffle

With larger needles and MC, use the long-tail cast-on method (see page 13) to CO 128 sts.

Beg with a knit row, work in St st for 10 rows.

Cut MC, leaving a generous tail for weaving in later.

Next row—dec row (RS): Change to smaller needles and CC and then k1, *k3tog; rep from * to last st, k1—44 sts.

Scarf Body

Rows 1–5: Still using smaller needles and CC, knit. Cut CC, leaving a generous tail.

Row 6—inc row (RS): Change to larger needles and MC and then k1, *kfb; rep from * to last st, k1—86 sts.

Rows 7 and 9: Purl.

Row 8: Knit.

Rows 10–15: Rep rows 8 and 9 three times more. Cut MC, leaving a generous tail.

Row 16—dec row (RS): Change to smaller needles and CC and then k1, *k2tog; rep from * to last st, k1—44 sts.

Repeat rows 1–16 until scarf measures approx 58 inches from CO edge, ending with row 16.

Still using smaller needles and CC, knit 5 rows. Cut CC, leaving a generous tail.

Ruffle

Next row (RS): With larger needles and MC, k1, *kfb&f; rep from * to last st, k1—128 sts.

Beg with a purl row, work in St st for 9 rows.

BO knitwise.

Finishing

Weave in ends.

Brocade Headband

Skill Level – Easy      *Designer – Sharon Turner*

Here's a small project that you can knit up quickly but that will hold your interest. It has a pretty brocade stitch pattern on the front, turned hems, and an easy stripe pattern on the underside. Small enough to pop into your purse, headbands and other small projects like this are great for knitters on the go.

specifications

Sizes

S (M, L)

Size shown: M

Finished Measurements

Circumference: 17½ (19, 20½) inches

Materials

- 1 ball GGH/Muench *Wollywasch* (100% wool, 136 yd./50 g ball) color #98 (MC) and 1 ball color #140 (CC)
- US 3 (3.25 mm) needles
- US 4 (3.5 mm) needles
- Tapestry needle

Gauge

22 sts and 28 rows to 4 inches in stockinette stitch on US 4 (3.5 mm) needles, or size needed to obtain gauge

Pattern Stitches
St st (Stockinette Stitch) Worked in Rows

Row 1 (RS): Knit.

Row 2 (WS): Purl.

Rep rows 1 and 2 for St st worked in rows.

Brocade Pattern (Mult of 8 Sts Plus 1) Worked in Rows

Row 1 (RS): K4, *p1, k7; rep from * to last 5 sts, p1, k4.

Rows 2 and 8 (WS): P3, *k1, p1, k1, p5; rep from * to last 6 sts, k1, p1, k1, p3.

Rows 3 and 7: K2, *p1, k3; rep from * to last 3 sts, p1, k2.

Rows 4 and 6: P1, *k1, p5, k1, p1; rep from * to end.

Row 5: *P1, k7; rep from * to last st, p1.

Rep rows 1–8 for brocade pattern worked in rows.

2 rows MC

2 rows CC

instructions

With smaller needles and CC, use the long-tail cast-on method (see page 13) to CO 97 (105, 113) sts.

Row 1 (RS): Knit.

Row 2 (WS): Purl.

Change to MC and work stripe patt over next 8 rows, ending with a WS row in CC.

Next row—turning ridge (RS): Still using CC, purl.

Next row (WS): Changing to larger needle and MC, purl.

Beg next row, work brocade patt in MC over 17 rows, ending with row 1 to complete patt evenly.

Change to CC and purl 1 row.

Next row—turning ridge (RS): Still using CC, change to smaller needle and purl.

Next row (WS): Still using CC, purl.

Change to MC and work stripe patt over next 8 rows, ending with a WS row in CC.

Still using CC, BO all sts.

Finishing

Weave in ends. Steam entire headband, unfolded, to block and reduce curling. Fold along the turning ridges and steam again to prepare for sewing seams.

Sew cast-on edge to bound-off edge using CC and an invisible horizontal seam (see page 63). Sew together ends to join in a circle, using MC and mattress stitch (see page 63) along the striped underside and the brocade front.

Steam again to neaten seams.

Chapter 14
fashionista

You're an avid follower of fashion—never a fashion victim—and you know how to put together a look. Instead of shopping, shopping, shopping, and potentially arriving at the party carrying the same bag or wearing the same skirt as one of your fashion-conscious friends, why not knit a few of your own one-of-a-kind styles? This chapter gives you patterns for a fun mini-skirt, an elegant little clutch, and a frou-frou stole. You might also like the Pretty in Pink scarf on page 121, the Ballet Shrug on page 104, and the Newsboy Cap on page 85.

Ruffle Skirt

Skill Level – Easy　　*Designer – Jill Draper*

Want something both comfortable *and* cute to wear? This skirt is for you. The soft and stretchy yarn makes a fabric that feels like your favorite sweats, and the short, ruffled style is easily dressed up or down. It looks great with leggings or textured tights; the more daring can wear it bare legged. This version sports ties made from twisted cords, but you could substitute grosgrain ribbons or skinny belts. Because this skirt is worked in the round, with the contrasting color carried up what will become the side seam, there is virtually no finishing required. Don't be intimidated by the enormous number of stitches in the last couple of rounds; it goes much faster than you may think, and there is no reason to count the stitches because being a stitch or two off won't make a huge difference.

specifications

Size

XS (S, M, L, XL)

Size shown: S

Finished Measurements

High hip circumference: 30 (33½, 36½, 40, 43½) inches

note: Measure your hip about 3 inches below your belly button, or wherever you want the waistline of the skirt to be.

Length: 14 (14, 14½, 14½, 15) inches

note: The version shown is a mini skirt, but the length can easily be adjusted by working more rows before the ruffle. Just be sure to purchase more yarn so you don't run out!

Materials

- 2 (2, 3, 3, 3) balls GGH/Muench *Esprit* (100% nylon, 87 yd./50 g ball) color #9 (MC) and 1 (1, 2, 2, 2) balls color #2 (CC)

- 10 yd. yarn to match CC for twisted cords

note: The sample shown used elann.com *Peruvian Highland Silk* (80% wool/20% silk, 122 yd./50 g ball) color #2055 for twisted cords.

- 10 yd. black–and–white marled yarn, or 10 yd. each black and white yarn for twisted cords

note: The sample shown used GGH/Muench *Davos Mouliné* (60% merino wool/40% acrylic, 96 yd./50 g ball) in color #1010 for twisted cords.

- US 9 (5.5 mm) 24–inch circular needle
- US 9 (5.5 mm) 40–inch circular needle
- Tapestry needle
- Stitch markers

Gauge

12 sts and 16 rows to 4 inches in stockinette stitch on US 9 (5.5 mm) needles, or size needed to obtain gauge

Pattern Stitches

St st (Stockinette Stitch) Worked in Rnds

Knit all rnds.

kfb (Knit into Front and Back)

Increase 1 st by knitting into the front and then into the back of the next st.

Color Stripe Pattern (Worked in St st)

8 rnds MC

1 rnd CC

note: Do not cut yarn when changing colors but carry CC up work as you go, twisting yarns together at beginning of every rnd.

instructions

Waistband

With shorter needle and CC, use long-tail cast-on method (see page 13) to CO 90 (100, 110, 120, 130) sts. Place marker to note beginning of rnd and join rnd, being careful not to twist sts.

Rnds 1 and 2: *K3, p2; rep from * to end.

Rnd 3—work eyelets: *K3, yo, p2tog; rep from * to end.

Rep rnd 1 until piece measures 1 inch from eyelet rnd.

Rep rnd 3 for second set of eyelets.

Rep rnd 1 until piece measures ½ inch from second eyelet rnd.

Skirt Body

Without cutting CC, join MC and begin working body of skirt in stripe patt. Rep stripe patt until skirt measures 13½ (13½, 14, 14, 14½) inches from CO edge, ending at any point in the stripe patt.

Ruffle

note: Change to the longer circular needle when the shorter one no longer accommodates the sts.

Next rnd: Using MC, *kfb; rep from * to end—180 (200, 220, 240, 260) sts.

Rep last rnd twice—720 (800, 880, 960, 1040) sts.

Next rnd: Changing to CC, *kfb; rep from * to end—1,440 (1,600, 1,760, 1,920, 2,080) sts.

BO all sts.

Finishing

Weave in ends.

Twisted Cord Ties

Cut each of the 10-yd. cord yarns into four 90-inch strands. Set two of the 90-inch strands of each color aside for the second cord. Hold the remaining four strands together and knot the ends. Attach one knotted end to a coat hook or a cabinet knob, pull the strands taut, and twist until the strands are tightly spun together. Maintaining tight tension on the strands, and taking care not to let them untwist, fold the strands in half—holding the fold loop firmly in one hand—so that the knotted ends are lined up with each other. Let go of the ends, and the cord twists itself together, forming an elegant rope. Rep for the second cord.

Weave cords through eyelet rows on waistband.

Designer Clutch

Skill Level – Intermediate  *Designer – Sharon Turner*

Use this compact bag to tote car keys, lipstick, and a few other small items to your next soirée. Even though the Fair Isle pattern looks complicated, it's not *too* difficult, and there's not much of it to knit. This bag is self-lined: You start by working one of the front panels, then you purl a turning ridge and work the lining on smaller needles, then purl another turning ridge and work the other outer panel. The handle is worked like a big buttonhole, so there's not a lot of finishing.

specifications

Size

One size

Finished Measurements

Width: 7½ inches

Height: 8 inches

Materials

- 2 balls elann.com *Peruvian Highland Silk* (80% wool/20% silk, 122 yd./50 g ball) color #2055 (A), 1 ball color #500 (B), and 1 ball color #0100 (C)
- US 5 (3.75 mm) needles
- US 6 (4 mm) needles
- US F (4 mm) crochet hook (optional)
- Tapestry needle
- Row counter

Gauge

21 sts and 24 rows to 4 inches in stockinette stitch on US 6 (4 mm) needles, or size needed to obtain gauge

Pattern Stitches

St st (Stockinette Stitch) Worked in Rows

Row 1 (RS): Knit.

Row 2 (WS): Purl.

Rep rows 1 and 2 for St st worked in rows.

note: The first and last sts on the chart are selvages, or edge sts. Work those only at the beginning and end of every row, working the 14-st repeat three times between the selvages.

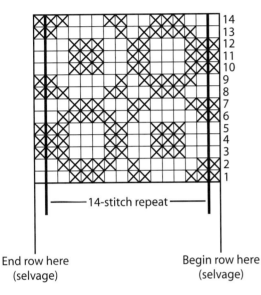

14-stitch repeat

End row here
(selvage)

Begin row here
(selvage)

instructions
Front Panel 1

With larger needles and B, use the long–tail cast–on method (see page 13) to CO 44 sts.

Using B and C, work Fair Isle patt from chart, beg with row 1, for 35 rows, ending with row 7, a RS row.

Cut B and C.

Next row (WS): Change to A and purl.

Beg with a knit row, work in St st for 4 rows.

Next row (RS)—handle: K14, BO 16, k14.

Next row (WS): P14, turn to RS and use cable cast–on method (see page 70, under "One–Row Horizontal Buttonhole") to CO 16, turn back to WS, p14.

Beg with a knit row, work in St st for 6 rows.

Lining

Next row (RS)—turning ridge: Change to smaller needles and purl.

Beg with a purl row, work in St st for 6 rows.

Next row (WS)—handle: P14, BO 16, p14.

Next row (RS): K14, turn to WS and use cable cast–on method (see page 70, under "One–Row Horizontal Buttonhole") to CO 16, turn back to RS, k14.

Beg with a purl row, work in St st until lining measures approximately 14½ inches from turning ridge, ending with a WS row.

note: If your row gauge is different from the one specified in this pattern, measure by folding the lining at the turning ridge and again at the point that matches up to the CO edge. Work until the lining is about ½ or ¼ inch below the first handle bind-off row, ending with a WS row.

Next row (RS)—handle: K14, BO 16, k14.

Next row (WS): P14, turn to RS and use the cable cast–on method (see page 70, under "One–Row Horizontal Buttonhole") to CO 16, turn back to WS, p14.

Beg with a knit row, work in St st for 6 rows.

Front Panel 2

Next row—turning ridge (RS): Purl.

Change to larger needles and, beg with a purl row, work in St st for 6 rows.

Next row—handle (RS): P14, BO 16, p14.

Next row (RS): K14, turn to WS and use the cable cast–on method (see page 70, under "One–Row Horizontal Buttonhole") to CO 16, turn back to RS, k14.

Beg with a purl row, work in St st for 5 rows. Cut A.

Join B and C, and beg with chart row 8 (a RS row), work 35 rows of chart, ending with chart row 14. Cut C.

Next row (WS): Using B only, purl.

BO all sts.

Finishing

Weave in ends. If your yarn's care instructions allow, lightly steam to block and eliminate curling.

Fold piece in half with RS facing each other (inside out), matching up CO and BO edges, and pinning each side at the turning ridge to hold in place.

Use mattress stitch (see page 63) to sew the lining and front and back panel seams on each side, starting at the base of the fold and ending at the CO and BO edges. Use A for lining seams and B for front and back panel seams.

Fold piece along turning ridges so that the right sides of the front and back panel face out and so the handle holes are lined up and the CO edge meets the BO edge at the base. Steam the turning ridge folds and the lining fold.

Using A, whipstitch (see page 76) or crochet slip stitch (see page 79) the front panel side of the handle hole together with the lining side of the handle hole. Rep for the other handle.

Using B, whipstitch (see page 76) the cast-on and bound-off edges together at the base.

Use B and straight stitch (see page 76) to decoratively stitch around the perimeter of each handle.

Steam to neaten, if desired and if your yarn's care instructions allow.

Variation

You know those preppy reversible and interchangeable bags with the wooden handles? Substitute a bright yellow, teal, and pink for the black, white, and red, and you'll have something remarkably similar to one of those.

If you're more of an arty type, try substituting cotton yarn in cornflower blue, lime or olive green, and orange for the three colors.

Mini Stole

Skill Level – Easy   *Designer – Sharon Turner*

Keep your neck warm in style with this weightless loop-stitch stole. Once you get the hang of making the loops, knitting this one is a walk in the park. It's actually a plain, shaping-free rectangle with gathered ends. Add a couple cords and pompoms, and you're done. Look for a super-light yarn that won't itch your neck.

specifications

Size

One size

Finished Measurements

Width: 7 inches

Length: 25 inches, not including ties

Materials

- 3 balls GGH/Muench *Soft-Kid* (70% super kid mohair/25% nylon/5% wool, 151 yd./25 g ball) color #004

note: A double strand of yarn is used for this project.

- US 17 (12 mm) needles
- US H (5 mm) crochet hook
- 1⅜ inch plastic pompom maker
- Tapestry needle
- Row counter

Gauge

8 sts and 8 rows to 4 inches in loop stitch on US 17 (12 mm) needles *using yarn held double*, or size needed to obtain gauge

note: If you decide to use different yarn to make this pattern, look for yarn that by itself has a gauge of 18 sts to 4 inches in stockinette stitch on US 5–6 (3.75–4.25 mm) needles.

Pattern Stitches

Loop 1

Insert right needle into next st on left needle knitwise, bring working yarn to front between needles and wrap it around right needle tip and the first two fingers of your left hand clockwise 3 times, then wrap the working yarn once more around the needle only; pull the 4 loops (wraps) partway through the st on the left needle and use the right needle to place them onto the left needle next to the same st, then knit together the 4 loops and the st as 1 st.

Loop Stitch (Mult of 2 Sts Plus 1)

Rows 1 and 3 (RS): Purl.

Row 2 (WS): Loop 1, *k1, loop 1; rep from * to end.

Row 4: K1, *loop 1, k1; rep from * to end.

Rep rows 1–4 for loop stitch.

instructions

Using a double strand of yarn and long–tail cast–on method (see page 13), CO 15 sts.

Beg with row 1, work in loop stitch until piece measures 24–25 inches, ending with a WS (loop) row. BO purlwise.

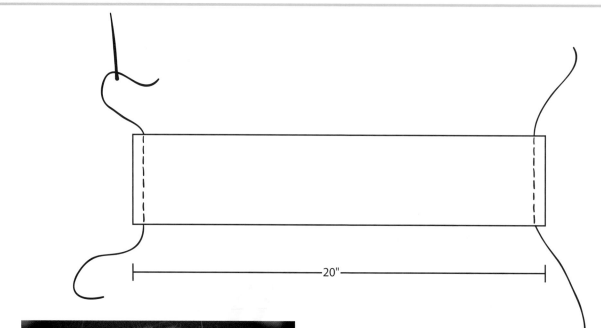

Finishing

Weave in ends.

Stole Ends

Using a tapestry needle threaded with a strand of the same yarn used for the stole, weave needle in and out along CO edge, as shown in illustration. Remove the tapestry needle and tie the yarn ends tightly together to gather the edge. Rep for the BO edge. Weave in the tied yarn ends.

Ties and Pompoms

Cut four strands of yarn 120 inches long. Set aside two of the strands for second tie. Hold together the other two strands and fold in half. Insert the crochet hook into the gathered end of the stole and pull through the loop formed by the folded strands. Yarn over the hook using the 4-strand-thickness of the strands and pull the new loop through the first loop to begin the chain. Continue working the chain until it is about 12 inches long. (See page 79 for instructions on crocheting a chain.) Cut the yarn, leaving an 8-inch tail; pull tail through last loop and tighten. Rep for the other end of the stole.

Use plastic pompom maker to form two 1⅜–1½ inch pompoms (see page 75). Sew a pompom to end of each tie.

Chapter 15
punk

Back in the 1970s, when punk was shocking and new, most people would not have associated handknits with the typically punk combat boots, chains, studs, spikes, and leather. But times have changed, and so has knitting's image. Knitting patterns and books geared toward punk style abound. Turn to this chapter to complete *your* punk look with skull wristbands, a long skinny striped scarf, and a mini kilt. Just add your own striped tights, chunky boots, and spiky 'do.

Skull Wristbands

Skill Level – Easy/Intermediate   *Designer – Sharon Turner*

Freak out your folks with these racy wristbands. Though small, these little bands pack in several fun techniques: Fair Isle, split-stitch embroidery, duplicate stitch, and seaming with mattress stitch. Try inventing your own embroidered motifs. Knitting these may become addictive, but that's okay because they'll look cool stacked several high up your forearm.

specifications

Size

S (M, L)

Sample shown: M

Finished Measurements

Circumference: 5 (6, 7) inches

Materials

- 1 ball Lion Brand *Lion Cashmere Blend* (72% merino/14% cashmere/14% nylon, 84 yd./40 g ball) color #135 (A) and 1 ball color #113 (B)

- US 7 (4.5 mm) needles

- Tapestry needle

- Embroidery needle and white or off-white embroidery floss for checkered wristband

- 3 yd. *Lion Cashmere Blend* in color #101 for duplicate stitch skull (C)

Gauge

20 sts and 24 rows to 4 inches in stockinette stitch on US 7 (4.5 mm) needles, or size needed to obtain gauge

Pattern Stitches

St st (Stockinette Stitch) Worked in Rows

Row 1 (RS): Knit.

Row 2 (WS): Purl.

Rep rows 1 and 2 for St st worked in rows.

Fair Isle Check Pattern (Worked in St st)

Row 1 (RS): K3 in B, *k2 in A, k2 in B; rep from * to last 3 sts, k3 in A.

Row 2 (WS): P3 in A, *p2 in B, p2 in A; rep from * to last 3 sts, p3 in B.

Row 3: K3 in A, *k2 in B, k2 in A; rep from * to last 3 sts, k3 in B.

Row 4: P3 in B, *p2 in A, p2 in B; rep from * to last 3 sts, p3 in A.

Rep rows 1–4 for Fair Isle check pattern.

instructions

Checkered Wristband

Using the long–tail cast-on method (see page 13) and A, CO 26 (30, 34) sts.

Knit 2 rows for edging. Without cutting A, join B and work Fair Isle check pattern as follows:

note: See page 48 for Fair Isle instructions.

Row 1 (RS): K3 in B, *k2 in A, k2 in B; rep from * to last 3 sts, k3 in A.

Row 2 (WS): P3 in A, *p2 in B, p2 in A; rep from * to last 3 sts, p3 in B.

Row 3: K3 in A, *k2 in B, k2 in A; rep from * to last 3 sts, k3 in B.

Row 4: P3 in B, *p2 in A, p2 in B; rep from * to last 3 sts, p3 in A.

Rep these 4 rows 2 times more, then rep rows 1–2 once (14 pattern rows total). Cut B.

Using A only, knit 3 rows. BO all sts.

Duplicate Stitch Wristband

Using the long–tail cast–on method (see page 13) and B, CO 27 (31, 35) sts.

note: Do not cut yarn when changing colors but carry color not in use up work as you go, twisting yarns together at the beginning of every row.

Row 1 (RS): Purl. Without cutting B, change to A.

Row 2 (WS): Knit. Without cutting A, change back to B.

Row 3: Purl. Cut B.

Using A only, and beg with a WS (purl) row, work 19 rows in St st. Without cutting A, change to B.

Next row (RS): Purl. Without cutting B, change to A.

Next row (WS): Knit. Cut A and work remainder in B only.

Next row: Purl.

BO all sts.

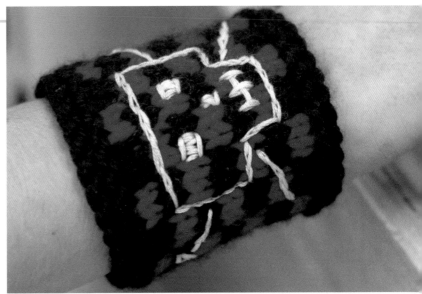

Finishing
Checkered Wristband

Weave in ends.

Using embroidery needle and floss, use split stitch (see below) to embroider skull onto center of wristband as shown.

Sew back seam 1 st in from side edges (to complete check pattern evenly) using mattress stitch (see page 63).

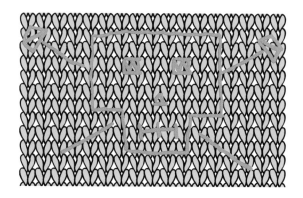

Duplicate Stitch Wristband

Weave in ends.

Use C and tapestry needle to work skull in duplicate stitch from chart, centering motif as evenly as possible between side edges and cast-on and bound-off edges. (See page 77 for duplicate stitch instructions.)

Sew back seam 1 st in from side edges using mattress stitch (see page 63).

Split stitch is an embroidery stitch that's good for outlines. It's kind of like backstitch (see page 65), except the stitches are shorter, and you split the stitches by bringing the needle directly through each stitch right after the backstitch. Here's how to do it:

1 Bring the threaded needle up through the fabric from back to front, and then insert the needle back into the fabric from front to back a short stitch away.

2 Bring the needle from back to front again, only this time bring it through the center of the stitch you just made, splitting the stitch.

Long Skinny Striped Scarf

Skill Level – Very Easy ☠ *Designer – Sharon Turner*

You produce this simple scarf's lively look with varying widths of high-contrast stripes. If you carry the yarns not in use up the side as you go, you'll have practically no finishing—just weave in the few ends from casting on, binding off, and joining a new ball, and then let the scarf curl. Wrap it around your neck several times for a stacked effect or just once to showcase the length.

specifications

Size

One size

Finished Measurements

Length: 68 inches

Width: 4¼ inches, uncurled

Materials

- 2 balls Lion Brand *Lion Cashmere Blend* (72% merino/14% cashmere/14% nylon, 84 yd./40 g ball) color #135 (A) and 2 balls color #101 (B)
- US 8 (5 mm) needles
- Row counter (optional)
- Tapestry needle

Gauge

17 sts and 25 rows to 4 inches in stockinette stitch on US 8 (5 mm) needles, or size needed to obtain gauge

Pattern Stitches

St st (Stockinette Stitch) Worked in Rows

Row 1 (RS): Knit.

Row 2 (WS): Purl.

Rep rows 1 and 2 for St st worked in rows.

instructions

Using the long-tail cast-on method (see page 13) and A, CO 20 sts. Slip a row counter onto your needle, if desired.

Beg with a knit row, work the entire scarf in St st in the following stripe patterns, twisting colors together every other row to carry the color not in use up the side.

For rows 1–20, rep the following 4-row stripe pattern:

2 rows A

2 rows B

For rows 21–36, rep the following 8-row stripe pattern:

4 rows A

4 rows B

For rows 37–60, rep the following 12-row stripe pattern:

6 rows A

6 rows B

Work rows 61–76 as follows:

8 rows A

8 rows B

Work rows 77–100 as follows:

12 rows A

12 rows B

Rep last 100 rows 3 times more (for a total of 400 rows from CO edge).

For rows 401–420, rep the following 4-row stripe pattern:

2 rows A

2 rows B

Change to A and work 2 final rows in St st.

Next row (RS): BO all sts.

Finishing

Weave in ends. Let the sides curl naturally.

Variation

You can make this easy scarf in any length and in any color and stripe combination. Wouldn't it be cool to knit two or three of these in different color schemes and wear them together? Or you could work one two-color scheme for the first half and change to a new scheme for the second half. Cinching the scarf ends together and sewing on a pompom is an easy makeover, too.

Striped Mini Kilt

Skill Level – Easy  *Designer – Sharon Turner*

This cute kilt is so easy to make: You just knit three panels in different stripe patterns and then sew two seams to join them into a wrap skirt. The kilt looks great with tights (even more stripes?) or over leggings. If you know how to sew, you might try lining your kilt, but it's not necessary.

specifications
Size
XS (S, M, L, XL)

Sample shown: S

Finished Measurements
Waist circumference: 28 (30, 32, 34, 36) inches

Length: 13 (13, 14, 14, 14½) inches

Materials
- 3 (3, 4, 4, 5) balls GGH/Muench *Savanna* (43% alpaca/ 23% linen/ 19% wool/15% nylon, 88 yd./50 g ball) color #025 (A) and 3 (3, 3, 4, 4) balls color #024 (B)
- US 10½ (6.5 mm) straight needles
- Row counter (optional)
- Tapestry needle
- 2 1-inch buttons
- US J (6 mm) crochet hook (optional)

Gauge
16 sts and 20 rows to 4 inches in stockinette stitch on US 10½ (6.5 mm) needles, or size needed to obtain gauge

Pattern Stitches
Garter Stitch Worked in Rows
Knit all rows.

St st (Stockinette Stitch) Worked in Rows
Row 1 (RS): Knit.

Row 2 (WS): Purl.

Rep rows 1 and 2 for St st worked in rows.

k2tog (Knit 2 Together)
Insert the right needle into the front of the next 2 sts on the left needle as if to knit. Wrap the yarn over the right needle and knit the 2 sts as 1 st.

yo (Yarn Over)
Bring the working yarn to the front of the needles and lay it over the right needle from front to back. This creates another st.

instructions
Back Panel
Back Panel Hem

Using the long-tail cast-on method (see page 13) and A, CO 72 (76, 80, 84, 88) sts. Slip a row counter onto your needle, if desired.

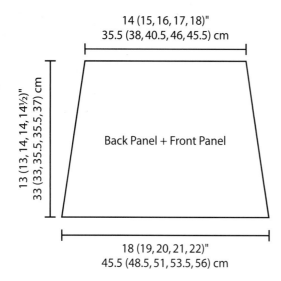

14 (15, 16, 17, 18)"
35.5 (38, 40.5, 46, 45.5) cm

13 (13, 14, 14, 14½)"
33 (33, 35.5, 35.5, 37) cm

Back Panel + Front Panel

18 (19, 20, 21, 22)"
45.5 (48.5, 51, 53.5, 56) cm

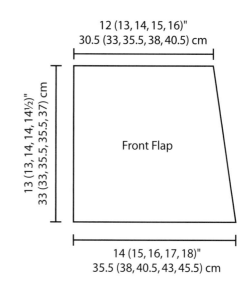

12 (13, 14, 15, 16)"
30.5 (33, 35.5, 38, 40.5) cm

13 (13, 14, 14, 14½)"
33 (33, 35.5, 35.5, 37) cm

Front Flap

14 (15, 16, 17, 18)"
35.5 (38, 40.5, 43, 45.5) cm

Work in garter st for 14 rows.

Back Panel Body

note: For all panels, stripe pattern and side shaping occur simultaneously, so be sure to read ahead before beginning stripe patterns.

Beg with a knit row, work the entire back panel body in St st in the following stripe pattern, twisting colors together every other row to carry the color not in use up the side.

For the next 48 (48, 52, 52, 56) rows, rep the following 12-row stripe pattern:

  4 rows B

  8 rows A

AT THE SAME TIME, shape sides by dec 1 st each end of the first row of the stripe pattern, then each end of every 8th row 2 (2, 4, 4, 6) times, then every 6th row 5 (5, 3, 3, 1) times—56 (60, 64, 68, 72) sts.

note: To shape sides, use a k2tog wherever the pattern indicates a decrease.

Back Panel Waistband

Change to B if not in use already and work in garter st for 9 rows. BO all sts knitwise.

Front Panel
Front Panel Hem

Using the long-tail cast-on method (see page 13) and A, CO 72 (76, 80, 84, 88) sts. Slip a row counter onto your needle, if desired.

Work in garter st for 14 rows.

Front Panel Body

Beg with a knit row, work the entire front panel body in St st in the following stripe pattern, twisting colors together every other row to carry the color not in use up the side.

For the next 48 (48, 52, 52, 56) rows, rep the following 6-row stripe pattern:

  4 rows B

  2 rows A

AT THE SAME TIME, shape sides by dec 1 st each end of the first row of the stripe pattern, then each end of every 8th row 2 (2, 4, 4, 6) times, then every 6th row 5 (5, 3, 3, 1) times—56 (60, 64, 68, 72) sts.

Front Panel Waistband

Change to B if not in use already and work in garter st for 9 rows. BO all sts knitwise.

Front Flap
Front Flap Hem

Using the long-tail cast-on method (see page 13) and A, CO 56 (60, 64, 68, 72) sts.

Work in garter st for 14 rows.

Front Flap Body

Beg with a knit row, work the entire front flap body in St st in the following stripe pattern, twisting colors together every other row to carry the color not in use up the side.

For the next 28 (28, 32, 32, 36) rows, work the following stripe pattern:

    8 rows B
    2 rows A
    2 rows B

Rep the last 4 rows (2 rows A, 2 rows B) 4 (4, 5, 5, 6) times.

For the next 20 rows, work the following stripe pattern:

    8 rows A
    4 rows B
    4 rows A
    4 rows B

AT THE SAME TIME, shape right edge by dec 1 st at the beginning of the first row of the stripe pattern, then at the beginning of every 8th row 2 (2, 4, 4, 6) times, then every 6th row 5 (5, 3, 3, 1) times—48 (52, 56, 60, 64) sts.

Front Flap Waistband

note: The front flap is shaped on the right edge only.

Change to A and work in garter st for 4 rows.

> **Next row—buttonholes (RS):** K4, yo, k2tog, knit to last 5 sts, k2tog, yo, k3.

Work in garter st for 4 rows more. BO all sts knitwise.

Finishing

Weave in ends.

Sew right edge of back panel to left edge of front panel using mattress stitch. (See page 63 for instructions.) Sew left edge of back panel to right edge of front flap using mattress stitch.

Slip stitch crochet left edge of front flap using A, if desired. (See page 79 for instructions.)

Block (see pages 60–62) if desired and if yarn manufacturer's care instructions allow.

Sew buttons to waistband of front panel to correspond with buttonholes on front flap.

Variations

If you're more into preppy than punk, try this kilt in pink and green or yellow and pink. Or how about accenting the left edge of the front flap with some short, bristly fringe—just like a real kilt? You can even use one of your metal stitch holders as a kilt pin!

Chapter 16

preppy

*I*f you're into that breezy, summery yacht club style—polo shirts, sporty accessories, pastel greens, yellows, and pinks—then this chapter is for you. You'll want to knit the adorable tennis socks, complete with pompoms, or the irresistible stretchy bobbled hat. Look the part with the braided belt (is that really knit?), or, if you're looking for a bigger project, try the preppy pastel sleeveless hoodie.

Don't limit yourself to this chapter alone. If you skipped over the punk chapter, you missed the striped kilt, which would look perfectly preppy if you replaced the black and gray with pink and green. And check out the Brocade Headband on page 123; that one is probably right up your alley, too.

Knit-to-Fit Tennis Socks

Skill Level – Intermediate ◈◈◈ *Designer – Heather Brack*

In pale yellow and leafy green, these anklets will add a touch of color to your tennis whites on the courts. The pom-poms on the back are retro-style fun and peek over the tops of your sneakers, and the stretchy cotton yarn ensures a snug and comfortable fit.

People are often concerned about whether they should try to work with stretchy yarn stretched or completely relaxed. The best advice is just to try not to overthink it. Let the yarn do what it wants, but be sure to check your gauge.

specifications

Size

One size

Finished Measurements

Circumference: stretchy; to fit women's US shoe size 6–10

Length: custom

Materials

- 2 balls Cascade Yarns *Fixation* (98.3% cotton/1.7% elastic, 100 yd. (relaxed)/50 g ball) color #1198 (MC) and 1 ball color #5185 (CC)
- US 3 (3.25 mm) double-pointed needles, set of 4
- Tapestry needle
- Stitch holder

Gauge

28 sts and 36 rows to 4 inches in stockinette stitch (unstretched) on US 3 (3.25 mm) needles, or size needed to obtain gauge

Pattern Stitches

Wrap 1 in a Knit Row

Sl 1 as if to purl (with yarn in front), bring yarn to back, turn work, sl 1 as if to purl (with yarn in front), bring yarn to back.

Wrap 1 in a Purl Row

Sl 1 as if to purl (with yarn in back), bring yarn to front, turn work, sl 1 as if to purl (with yarn in back), bring yarn to front.

St st (Stockinette Stitch) Worked in Rnds

Knit all rnds.

2 x 1 Rib (Mult of 3 Sts) Worked in Rnds

Rnd 1: *K2, p1; rep from * to end.

Rep rnd 1 for 2 x 1 rib worked in rnds.

Knit tbl (Knit Through Back Loop)

Knit through the back loop.

note: These socks are worked a little differently than most—even for socks worked from the toe up. The contrast color toe seam is the cast-on row; from there you shape the toe to the tip with short-rowing. After you work the toe, you pick up the instep stitches from the contrast color cast-on edge, join the round, and then work through the foot and heel in the usual toe-up fashion.

instructions

Toe

Using CC and backward–loop method (see page 13), CO 30 sts to a dpn. Cut CC, leaving a 6–inch tail.

Join MC and knit 1 row.

Begin short rows as follows:

note: For a refresher on short-rowing, see page 35.

Row 1 (WS): P29, wrap 1.
Row 2 (RS): K28, wrap 1.
Row 3: P27, wrap 1.
Row 4: K26, wrap 1.

Continue working wraps in this manner, with 1 fewer st before the wrap in each row, until only 8 sts remain in the center section between wraps. Then pick up wraps as follows, working each wrap together with its wrapped st:

Row 1 (WS): P8, pick up and purl wrap together with next st, turn.
Row 2 (RS): K9, pick up and knit wrap together with next st, turn.
Row 3: P10, pick up and purl wrap together with next st, turn.
Row 4: K11, pick up and knit wrap together with next st, turn.

Continue in this manner, knitting or purling to the wrapped st on each row and working the wrap together with the st, until all wraps have been picked up.

Toe Seam

With 2 more dpns, pick up and knit tbl 30 sts from the CO edge—60 sts total. Arrange your sts so you have 15 on each of 2 needles (for the instep) and 30 on a third needle (for the sole).

note: The CC toe seam is on the 30 instep sts.

Foot

Work the 60 sts in the round in St st until sock reaches the base of ankle when tried on, without stretching.

Knit 3 more rnds.

Place the 30 instep sts on a holder.

Heel

Work the 30 heel sts as follows:

Row 1: P29, wrap 1.
Row 2: K28, wrap 1.
Row 3: P27, wrap 1.
Row 4: K26, wrap 1.

Continue working wraps in this manner, with 1 fewer st before the wrap each row, until 8 sts remain in the center section between wraps. Then pick up wraps as follows, working the wrap together with each wrapped st:

Row 1 (WS): P8, pick up and purl wrap together with next st, turn
Row 2 (RS): K9, pick up and knit wrap together with next st, turn
Row 3: P10, pick up and purl wrap together with next st, turn.
Row 4: K11, pick up and knit wrap together with next st, turn.

Continue in this manner, knitting or purling to the wrapped st on each row and working the wrap together with the st, until all wraps have been picked up.

Edging

When heel is complete, put the reserved instep sts back on the needles.

Knit 3 rnds. Cut MC, leaving a 6–inch tail.

Join CC and knit 1 rnd.

Work 3 rnds in 2 x 1 rib. BO in patt.

Make second sock same as the first.

Finishing

Weave in ends.

Block by soaking in cold water for at least 10 minutes to allow yarn to relax. Lay flat to dry.

For each sock, make a pompom with CC. (See page 75 for pompom instructions.) Sew pompom to heel.

Braided Linen Belt

Skill Level – Intermediate   ◈◈◈   *Designer – Heather Brack*

A ribbon belt looks great with jeans and a t-shirt or can brighten up a pair of khakis. Once you get the hang of the braided basket stitch, it goes pretty quickly. You may want to make this belt in several different colors.

specifications

Size

XS (S, M, L, XL)

Size shown: XS

Finished Measurements

29 (32½, 36½, 40, 44) inches

Materials

* 1 ball Louet *Euroflax Sport Weight* (100% linen, 270 yd./100 g ball) color #04 (A), 1 ball color #62 (B), and 1 ball color #27 (C)
* US 3 (3.25 mm) straight needles
* Tapestry needle
* 2 1¾-inch D-rings

Gauge

21½ sts and 36 rows to 4 inches in braided basket stitch on US 3 (3.25 mm) needles, or size needed to obtain gauge

Pattern Stitches

Braided Basket Stitch

Row 1 (RS): *Insert right needle from back to front between first 2 sts on left needle, knit the second st, pull right needle out from between sts (keeping the new loop on the needle), and knit the first st, drop both sts from the left needle; rep from * to end.

Row 2: (WS): P1, *purl the second st on the left needle, purl the first st on the left needle, slip both sts from the left needle together; rep from * to last st, p1.

Rep rows 1–2 for braided basket stitch.

instructions

Using A and long-tail cast-on method (see page 13), CO 160 (180, 202, 220, 242) sts.

Knit 1 row. Cut A.

Join B and knit 2 rows.

Work 2 rows in braided basket patt, beg with row 1. Cut B.

Join A and work 1 row in braided basket patt. Cut A.

Join C and work 4 rows in braided basket patt. Cut C.

Join A and work 1 row in braided basket patt. Cut A.

Join B and work 2 rows in braided basket patt.

Knit 2 rows. Cut B.

Join A and knit 1 row.

BO all sts knitwise with A.

Finishing

Weave in ends; try to weave them into the edges of the belt as much as possible so they don't show through the braided pattern.

Pass one end of belt through both D-rings, fold about 1 inch of belt to WS, and stitch in place.

Preppy Bobbled Hat

Skill Level – Easy/Intermediate ✦✦✦ *Designer – Kitty Wilson Jarrett*

This fun preppy hat is basically just a tube, cinched at the top with a crocheted chain. Thanks to the elastic in the yarn and the cinched top, the hat shapes itself to your head, so you don't have to bother with decreasing at the top or switching to double-pointed needles. You'll find that making bobbles and working with multiple colors are easy techniques that add a lot of interest to your knitting.

specifications

Size
One size

Finished Measurements
Circumference (unstretched): 16 inches

Materials
- 1 ball elann.com *Esprit* (98.3% cotton/1.7% elastic, 100 yd. (unstretched)/50 g ball) color #6287 (A), 1 ball color #3703 (B), and 1 ball color #5606 (C)
- US 6 (4 mm) 16–inch circular needle
- Stitch marker
- US G (4.5 mm) crochet hook
- Tapestry needle

Gauge
20 sts and 38 rows to 4 inches in stockinette stitch (unstretched) on US 6 (4 mm) needles, or size needed to obtain gauge

Pattern Stitches
St st (Stockinette Stitch) Worked in Rnds
Knit all rnds.

mb (Make Bobble)
Knit into the front, back, front, back, and front (that's five times) of the next st. Without turning work, use the left needle to pick up the fourth st and pass it over the fifth and off the needle; pass the third st over the fifth and off the needle; pass the second st over the fifth and off the needle; and finally, pass the first st over the fifth and off the needle.

Rnd 1: *P1, k3; rep from * to end.

Rep rnd 1 for 1 x 3 rib.

k2tog (Knit 2 Together)

Insert the right needle into the front of the next 2 sts on the left needle as if to knit. Wrap the yarn over the right needle and knit the 2 sts as 1 st.

yo (yarn over)

Bring the working yarn to the front of the needles and lay it over the right needle from front to back. This creates another st.

instructions

Using A and the long–tail cast-on method (see page 13), CO 84 sts, place marker to note beginning of rnd, and join round, being careful not to twist sts.

Knit 2 rnds. Cut A, leaving a 6-inch tail.

Bobbles and Ribbing

Join B and knit 1 rnd.

Next rnd—bobbles: *K1, mb; rep from * to end.

Work 9 rnds in 1 x 3 rib.

Next rnd—bobbles: *K1, mb; rep from * to end. Cut B, leaving a 6-inch tail.

Two-Color Work

Join A and knit 3 rnds. Do not cut A.

Join C and begin two–color work as follows:

Rnds 1 and 7: *K3 in A, k1 in C; rep from * to end.

Rnds 2 and 6: K2 in A, *k1 in C, k3 in A; rep from * to last st, k1 in A.

Rnds 3 and 5: K1 in A, *k1 in C, k3 in A; rep from * to last 2 sts, k2 in A.

Rnd 4: *K1 in C, k3 in A; rep from * to end. Cut C, leaving a 6-inch tail.

Top of Hat

Continuing in A, work in St st until hat measures 7 inches from CO edge.

Next rnd—eyelets for crocheted chain: *K2tog, yo, k5; rep from * to end of rnd.

Knit 5 rnds more in A. Do not cut A.

Join C and knit 1 rnd. Cut C, leaving a 6-inch tail.

Knit 2 rnds in A. Do not cut A.

Join B and knit 1 rnd.

Next rnd—bobbles: *K1, mb; rep from * to end.

Cut B, leaving a 6-inch tail.

Knit 2 rnds in A.

Using A, BO all sts purlwise.

Finishing

Weave in ends.

Crochet Chain

Holding 2 strands of A together, crochet a chain 20 inches long. (See page 79 for crochet chain instructions.) Cut yarn ends and weave into chain. Thread crocheted chain through eyelets at top of hat, cinch tight, and tie in a bow.

Preppy Hoodie

Skill Level – Intermediate ✦✦✦ *Designer – Sharon Turner*

Great for the beach or over a long-sleeved tee, this sleeve-less hoodie is a cinch to make. You knit the stripe pattern by holding 2 colors of yarn together for each stripe. You can avoid having to weave in a lot of ends later by carrying the yarns not in use up the side—just twist the working yarns under the yarns not in use at the beginning of every RS row to carry them along.

specifications

Size

S (M, L)

Size shown: S

Finished Measurements

Chest circumference: 36 (40, 44) inches

Length: 21 (22, 23) inches

Materials

✦ 2 (3, 3) balls each Debbie Bliss *Pure Cotton* (100% cotton, 96 yd./50g ball) color #39005 (A), color #39004 (B), color #39008 (C), color #39012 (D), and color #39007 (E)

note: A double strand of yarn is used for this project.

✦ US 10½ (6.5 mm) straight needles

✦ US 10½ (6.5 mm) 24–inch circular needle for working hood and edgings

✦ US 10 (6 mm) double–pointed needles for joining shoulders, set of 3

✦ Tapestry needle

✦ 6 stitch holders

Gauge

12 sts and 18 rows to 4 inches in stockinette stitch *using yarn held double* on US 10½ (6.5 mm) needles, or size needed to obtain gauge

note: If you decide to use different yarn to make this pattern, look for yarn that by itself has a gauge of 18 sts to 4 inches in stockinette stitch on US 8 (5 mm) needles.

Pattern Stitches

St st (Stockinette Stitch) Worked in Rows

Row 1 (RS): Knit.

Row 2 (WS): Purl.

Rep rows 1 and 2 for St st worked in rows.

k2tog (Knit 2 Together)

Insert the right needle into the front of the next 2 sts on the left needle as if to knit. Wrap the yarn over the right needle and knit the 2 sts as 1 st.

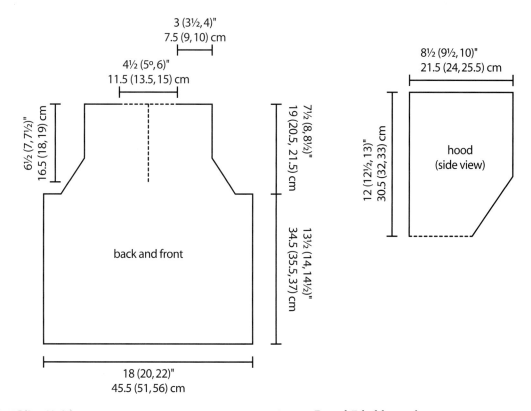

3 (3½, 4)"
7.5 (9, 10) cm

4½ (5°, 6)"
11.5 (13.5, 15) cm

6½ (7, 7½)"
16.5 (18, 19) cm

7½ (8, 8½)"
19 (20.5, 21.5) cm

13½ (14, 14½)"
34.5 (35.5, 37) cm

back and front

18 (20, 22)"
45.5 (51, 56) cm

8½ (9½, 10)"
21.5 (24, 25.5) cm

12 (12½, 13)"
30.5 (32, 33) cm

hood
(side view)

ssk (Slip, Slip, Knit)

Insert the right needle from front to back into the front of the next st on the left needle and slip it onto the right needle. Rep this with the next st. (You have slipped 2 sts knitwise from the left needle to the right needle.) Insert the left needle into the fronts of both slipped sts and then knit them as 1 st.

m1 (make 1)

Increase 1 st by using the left needle to pick up the horizontal strand from front to back between the last st worked on the right needle and the next st to be worked on the left needle and knit into the picked-up strand.

Stripe Pattern (Worked in St st)

4 rows C and D held together

4 rows E and A held together

4 rows B and C held together

4 rows D and E held together

4 rows A and B held together

Rep these 20 rows for stripe pattern.

instructions

Back

With straight needles and with A and B held together, use the long-tail method (see page 13) to CO 54 (60, 66) sts.

Knit 3 rows.

Next row (WS): Purl. Do not cut A and B.

Change to C and D, and beginning with a knit row, work in St st and stripe pattern, twisting colors together every other row to carry the colors not in use up the side, until back measures 13½ (14, 14½) inches from CO edge, ending with a WS row.

Put each set of shoulder sts onto a stitch holder and set aside.

Front

Work as for back, including armhole shaping.

> AT THE SAME TIME, when 42 (48, 54) sts rem, ending with a WS row, divide for front neck opening as follows:
>
> **Next row (RS):** K2tog, k19 (22, 25), put rem sts (which are for the right front) on holder or spare needle for later.

note: When a sweater or vest pattern refers to a left front or a right front, it means the *wearer's* left or right.

Work rem of left front armhole shaping as for back to 16 (19, 21) sts. Continue without further shaping until left front measures same as back, ending at the same WS row in the stripe pattern.

> **Next row (RS):** K9 (11, 12) for shoulder and put on holder, knit rem 7 (8, 9) sts for front of hood and put on second holder.

Rejoin yarn to right front sts with RS facing and complete right front as for left, except slip the shoulder sts onto one of the double-pointed needles and put the hood sts onto a holder.

Hood

Before working the hood, the shoulder seams must be joined. Put the right back shoulder sts onto another double-pointed needle. Holding the needle with the right front shoulder sts and the needle with the right back shoulder sts together, with RS facing each other, use a third double-pointed needle and the three-needle bind-off (see page 67) to join the shoulder seam. Rep for the left shoulder seam.

Turn RS out. Using circular needle and appropriate yarn for stripe patt, knit across the 7 (8, 9) sts from holder for right front, pick up and knit 18 (20, 22) sts across right shoulder seam, back neck, and left shoulder seam, then knit the 7 (8, 9) sts from holder for left front—32 (36, 40) sts.

Armhole Shaping

Continuing in St st and stripe patt, BO 5 sts beg next 2 rows.

Dec 1 st each end every RS row 6 (6, 7) times—32 (38, 42) sts.

note: To shape the armhole after the bind-off, begin every RS row with ssk, and end every RS row with k2tog, for the number of rows specified for the size being knit.

Continue in St st and stripe patt without further shaping until back measures 21 (22, 23) inches from CO edge, ending with the second row of any color stripe.

> **Next row (RS):** K9 (11, 12) for first shoulder, BO center 14 (16, 18) sts for neck, k9 (11, 12) for second shoulder. Cut yarn.

Maintaining stripe patt, purl 1 row.

Next row (RS): K3, m1, knit to last 3 sts, m1, k3—34 (38, 42) sts.

Work even in St st for 3 rows, maintaining stripe pattern.

Rep last 4 rows 9 times—52 (56, 60) sts.

Work without further shaping until hood measures 12 (12½, 13) inches from first hood row.

Place half the hood sts onto a second needle. Holding each set of hood sts with the right sides facing each other and needles parallel, join the hood top seam using the three-needle bind-off as you did for the shoulder seams.

Finishing

Weave in ends.

Armhole Edgings

note: Even though you use a circular needle to pick up and work the armhole edgings, the edgings are worked in rows. The circular needle makes picking up stitches along a curved edge a little easier.

With RS facing, using circular needle and C and E held together and, beginning at back right armhole edge, pick up and k27 (29, 31) sts up to shoulder seam, then pick up and k27 (29, 31) sts down right front armhole edge—54 (58, 62) sts.

Knit 1 row.

BO all sts knitwise.

Rep for left armhole edging.

Neck/Hood Trim

With RS facing, using circular needle and C and E held together and beg at base of neck opening on right front, pick up and k54 (58, 62) sts up neck opening and hood edge to hood top seam, then pick up and k54 (58, 62) sts back down left front of hood opening to base of neck opening—108 (116, 124) sts.

Knit 1 row.

BO knitwise. Cut yarn, leaving a 10-inch tail.

Final Assembly

Thread tail through a tapestry needle and stitch base of neck opening together to neaten it up.

Use mattress stitch (see page 63) to sew side seams, including armhole edgings.

Weave in rem ends.

Lightly steam to neaten seams and edgings, if desired and if yarn's care instructions allow.

hippie

Would you describe your favorite clothes as flowing and natural, beaded and lacy, tie–dyed and colorful? If so, you're lucky to be knitting now. Natural–fiber yarns spun from hemp, flax, and linen abound; colorful, hand–dyed, handspun, and variegated yarns in all the colors of the rainbow are easy to find.

This chapter offers a long, breezy open–work scarf, knit in yarn that has built–in color changes, a multicolored kerchief, also in self–patterning yarn, and a woven-looking bag that's fun to knit. You might also like the Newsboy Cap on page 85 and Hip Hip Belt on page 88. The Marly Mittens on page 99 are worth a look, too.

Extra-Long Scarf

Skill Level – Easy  *Designer – Sharon Turner*

This very long scarf has a nice loose drape to it—partly because the yarn is soft and supple, and partly because you knit it with needles a few sizes larger than the yarn specifies. You don't have to worry too much about gauge here; just get some soft yarn that will feel good on your neck and that will knit to a relaxed fabric. The lace pattern is almost effortless—you work the same row over and over again. Also, you don't have to buy extra yarn for the fringe if you have a lot of leftovers from other projects.

specifications

Size
One size

Finished Measurements
Length: 90 inches, not including fringe

Materials
- ☮ 3 balls Cascade Yarns/Di.Vé *Autunno* (100% merino wool, 98 yd./50 g ball) color #32965 (A)
- ☮ 1 skein Cascade Yarns *220 Quatro* (100% Peruvian highland wool, 220 yd./100 g skein) color #9433 (B)
- ☮ 1 skein Cascade Yarns *109* (100% Peruvian high-land wool, 109 yd./100 g skein) color #0294 (C)

note: Yarn A specifies a US 10¹/₂ (6.5 mm) needle; a needle two sizes larger is used for the scarf to ensure a relaxed fabric. Yarns B and C are for the fringe, but you can substitute yarn in any weight or color from your stash.

- ☮ US 13 (9 mm) needles
- ☮ Crochet hook (preferably larger than US G (4.5 mm) for adding fringe
- ☮ Tapestry needle

Gauge
10 sts and 12 rows to 4 inches in lacy rib stitch on US 13 (9 mm) needles, or size needed to obtain gauge

Pattern Stitches
Lacy Rib Stitch (Mult of 5 Sts Plus 6) Worked in Rows

Row 1 (RS): K3, *yo, k2tog, k1, p1, k1; rep from * to last 3 stitches, k2tog, k1.

Rep row 1 for lacy rib stitch worked in rows.

yo (Yarn Over)
Bring the working yarn to the front of the needles and lay it over the right needle from front to back. This creates another st.

k2tog (Knit 2 Together)

Insert the right needle into the front of the next 2 sts on the left needle as if to knit. Wrap the yarn over the right needle and knit the 2 sts as 1 st.

instructions

Using the long-tail CO method (see page 13) and A, CO 21 sts.

Knit 2 rows.

Beg working lacy rib pattern, as follows:

> **Row 1 (RS):** K3, *yo, k2tog, k1, p1, k1; rep from * to last 3 stitches, k2tog, k1.

Rep row 1 until scarf measures 90 inches from CO edge.

Knit 1 row.

BO all sts knitwise.

Finishing

Weave in ends.

Lightly steam to block, if necessary and if yarn's care instructions allow, using the instructions on pages 60–62. (The sample shown was not blocked.)

Make Fringe

For each bunch of fringe, cut two 15–inch strands each of yarns B and C. Hold the 4 strands together, fold in half, and use crochet hook to pull the fold loop through one corner of one of the scarf ends. Knot the ends through the loop and tighten. (See page 72 for fringe instructions.) Attach 8 bunches of fringe across each scarf end. Trim ends evenly.

Colorful Kerchief

Skill Level – Easy  *Designer – Sharon Turner*

Here's a fun accessory that you can knit up in a couple hours. It's a good way to practice shaping, if you haven't done much of that yet. A yarn-over at the beginning of each row shapes the triangle and at the same time produces a pretty line of eyelets along the edges. The sample here has a crocheted edging, but if you're not comfortable with crochet, you can omit that step and still end up with a cute bandana-like head covering.

specifications

Size

One size

Finished Measurements

Width at top: 16 inches

Length: 12 inches

Materials

- 1 ball elann.com *Sonata Print* (100% mercerized cotton, 115 yd./50 g ball) color #9776
- US 6 (4 mm) needles
- Tapestry needle
- US G (4.5 mm) crochet hook (optional)

Gauge

20 sts and 24 rows to 4 inches in stockinette stitch on US 6 (4 mm) needles, or size needed to obtain gauge

Pattern Stitches

St st (Stockinette Stitch) Worked in Rows

Row 1 (RS): Knit.

Row 2 (WS): Purl.

Rep rows 1 and 2 for St st worked in rows.

yo (Yarn Over)

Bring the working yarn to the front of the needles and lay it over the right needle from front to back. This creates another st.

k2tog (Knit 2 Together)

Insert the right needle into the front of the next 2 sts on the left needle as if to knit. Wrap the yarn over the right needle and knit the 2 sts as 1 st.

instructions

Using the long–tail CO method (see page 13), CO 2 sts.

> **Row 1 (RS):** K1, yo, k1—3 sts.
> **Row 2 (WS):** Knit.

Row 3: K1, yo, knit to end—4 sts.

Row 4: K1, yo, purl to end—5 sts.

Rep last 2 rows until you have 79 sts.

Next row—eyelet band (RS):
K1, *yo, k2tog; rep from * to end.

BO all sts knitwise.

Finishing

Weave in ends.

Lightly steam to block and reduce curling, if yarn's care instructions allow, using the instructions on pages 60–62.

Make Ties

For each tie, cut a strand of yarn 120 inches long. Fold the strand in half. Insert the crochet hook into one of the corners of the bound-off edge and pull through the loop formed by the folded strand. Yarn over the hook with the 2-strand thickness created by the folded strand and pull the new double loop through the first loop to begin the chain. Continue working the chain until it is about 12 inches long. (See page 79 for more instructions on crocheting a chain.) Cut the yarn, leaving an 8-inch tail; pull tail through last loop and tighten. Rep for tie at other corner.

Crochet Trim (Optional)

If desired, you can work a crochet trim around the two sides of the kerchief. With RS facing and beg at the top-left corner eyelet (where one of the ties is attached), insert the crochet hook, yarn over, and pull a loop through. *Chain 5, insert hook into the eyelet that is 2 to the left from the first (skip 1 eyelet), yarn over, pull the loop through the eyelet, yarn over again, pull this last loop through the 2 loops on the hook; rep from * around the perimeter of the triangle until you get to the second tie. Cut yarn, leaving a 6-inch tail; pull tail through last loop and tighten.

Weave in rem ends.

Lightly steam again to block and reduce curling.

Keep Knitting, and Your Kerchief Will Be a Shawl

If you just keep working the kerchief past the 12-inch mark, eventually it will start to look like a shawl. You'll need a lot more yarn to do this, so if that's your plan, purchase accordingly. To end up with a shawl that's about 25–30 inches long from the point to the top edge, you'll need at least 5 or 6 more balls of the yarn specified.

Suede Bag

Skill Level – Intermediate  **Designer – Sharon Turner**

This bag—perfect for carrying a wallet, keys, and a few other small essentials—isn't *really* suede; it's just made in yarn that looks kind of like suede. At first glance, you might think this is a woven bag rather than a knit one. That's the magic of linen stitch—slipping every other stitch every row creates this tightly woven fabric. (You actually use needles larger than your yarn calls for to work it, and you still end up with a gauge that is more stitches per inch than if you were knitting on needles of the size specified on the ball band.) There's a lot of fun in the details: After knitting an easy striped linen stitch rectangle, you crochet the seams and trim in an accent color, then you knit a ball for the button and work a long drop-stitch strap.

specifications

Size

One size

Finished Measurements

Width: 8 inches

Height: 9 inches, not including strap

Materials

- 1 skein Lion Brand *Lion Suede* (100% polyester, 122 yd./85 g skein) color #32 (A), 1 skein color #178 (B), and 1 skein color #147 (C)
- US 11 (8 mm) needles
- US 8 (5 mm) needles
- US 7 (4.5 mm) double–pointed needles, set of 4
- US H (5 mm) crochet hook
- Tapestry needle
- 2 cotton balls or a small handful of polyester fill (to stuff button)

Gauge

14 sts and 21 rows to 4 inches in linen stitch on US 11 (8 mm) needles, or size needed to obtain gauge

note: The generic gauge for this yarn is 12 stitches and 19 rows to 4 inches in stockinette stitch on US 8 (5 mm) needles.

Pattern Stitches

Linen Stitch (Mult of 2 Sts) Worked in Rows

Row 1 (RS): *K1, bring yarn to front, sl 1 st purlwise with yarn in front, bring yarn to back; rep from * to last 2 sts, k2.

Row 2 (WS): *P1, bring yarn to back, sl 1 st purlwise with yarn in back, bring yarn to front; rep from * to last 2 sts, p2.

Rep rows 1 and 2 for linen stitch worked in rows.

kfb (Knit into Front and Back)

Increase 1 st by knitting into the front and then into the back of the next st.

m1 (make 1)

Increase 1 st by using the left needle to pick up the horizontal strand from front to back between the last st worked on the right needle and the next st to be worked on the left needle and knit into the picked-up strand.

k2tog (Knit 2 Together)

Insert the right needle into the front of the next 2 sts on the left needle as if to knit. Wrap the yarn over the right needle and knit the 2 sts as 1 st.

Drop Stitch (Any Number of Sts) Worked in Rows

Rows 1 and 2: Knit.

Row 3 (RS): K1, *(yo) 3 times, k1; rep from * to end.

Row 4: K1, *push the 3 yo loops off the left needle and drop them, k1; rep from * to end.

note: Pull down on the CO edge after every 4th row to straighten the dropped stitches.

Rep rows 1–4 for drop stitch worked in rows.

instructions
Bag Body

With larger straight needles and A, use the long-tail CO method (see page 13) to CO 28 sts.

Beg with row 1, work in linen stitch for 4 rows. Do not cut A.

Change to B and, beg with row 1, work in linen stitch for 4 rows. Do not cut B.

note: Twist colors together every other row to carry the color not in use up the side.

Rep the last 8 rows until the piece measures approximately 23½ inches from beg, ending with the second row of either color's 4-row stripe.

> **Next row—buttonhole (RS):** Work in patt over first 11 sts, BO 6 stitches in patt, work in patt to end.

> **Next row (WS):** Work in patt over first 11 sts, CO 6 stitches using backward-loop cast-on method (see page 13), continue in patt as established to end.

Work 6 rows in patt, switching colors as appropriate.

> **Next row (RS):** K1, bring yarn to front, sl 1 purl-wise with yarn in front, pass 1st st over 2nd and off; beg with a k1, work in linen st patt to last 2 sts, k2tog.

> **Last row (WS):** *Sl 1 with yarn in back, bring yarn to front, p1, pass 1st st over 2nd and off, bring yarn to back; rep from * to end, binding off all sts in patt. Cut yarn, leaving a 6-inch tail, pull through last stitch, and tighten.

Knitted Ball Button

Using C and the long-tail CO method (see page 13), CO 8 sts to a dpn. Divide the stitches as evenly as possible over 3 dpns. Place marker to note beginning of rnd and join round, being careful not to twist sts.

Rnd 1: *Kfb; rep from * to end—16 sts.

Rnds 2–4: Knit.

Rnd 5: K1, m1, *k2, m1; rep from * to last st, k1—24 sts.

Rnds 6 and 7: Knit.

Rnd 8: *K2tog; rep from * to end—12 sts.

Rep round 8 once more—6 sts.

Cut yarn, leaving an 8-inch tail.

With sts still on needles, stuff cotton balls or polyester fill through top to stuff the button. Pull yarn tail through rem 6 sts and tighten to close top. Weave in tail, pulling it down through the ball to conceal.

Thread tail left from casting on through the tapestry needle and weave it in and out along the CO edge. Cinch tight and secure to close up bottom. Leave this tail to sew the ball to the bag.

Drop Stitch Strap

With smaller straight needles and C, use the long-tail CO method (see page 13) to CO 5 sts, leaving at least an 8-inch tail.

Beg with row 1, work in drop stitch until strap measures approximately 45 inches, ending with row 1 or 2 of patt.

Bind of all sts knitwise. Cut yarn, leaving an 8-inch tail; pull tail through last st and tighten.

Leave tails from casting on and binding off for sewing handle to bag.

Finishing

Weave in ends on bag body. Measure 9 inches from CO edge and fold from that point with WS together, creating a 9-inch-high pocket.

Side Seam Crochet

Holding CO corner to side edge, with front panel facing, use a crochet hook and C to slip stitch crochet left seam through both thicknesses from CO edge down to fold. (See page 79 for slip stitch crochet instructions.)

Slip stitch crochet right seam in C with the front panel facing, starting at the fold edge and working up to the CO edge.

Flap Edge Crochet

With RS of flap facing and beg where right seam left off, work slip stitch crochet edging in C around perimeter of flap, ending where left seam began.

Weave in crochet ends.

Strap and Button Assembly

Use tails to neatly sew handle to inside top corners of bag.

Sew knitted ball button to front panel about 3½ inches up from fold at base of bag.

Contributing Designers

Heather Brack is an editor, a knitter, and a spinner who lives in downtown Cleveland with her dog, Black Francis. She designs knitted and felted accessories for people, pets, and wizards. Her patterns appear in many books, including *Felt Frenzy* and *Charmed Knits*.

Jill Draper has been knitting and crafting since she was a child. Jill's grandmother shared with Jill her love of craft and constant desire to be "doing something." Jill lives in Brooklyn, surrounded by yarn, rovings, buttons, fabric, and a spinning wheel, and she's pretty sure her studio still has walls and a floor, although she hasn't seen them in a really long time. You can see what she's been working on lately at www.jilldraper.net.

Regrettably, **Kitty Wilson Jarrett** didn't learn to knit until the tail end of her teen years. A friend taught her the basics in college, and today, she knits for her son, nieces and nephews, and friends—and sometimes herself. Kitty lives in Florida and is a freelance editor who often gets to work on knitting books. She makes time every week for knitting with friends.

Claudine Monique is defiantly smitten with knittin'. She began knitting as a child, making only small garter stitch projects. She relearned to knit in 2000 and now knits every second possible of every day. Claudine is a regular fixture of the New York City SnB. She enjoys making knitwear for her friends, family, and herself. You can check out her WIPs on her blog, smittenwknittin.blogspot.com.

Shannon Okey is the author of *Knitgrrl*, *Knitgrrl 2*, *Spin to Knit*, *Crochet Style*, and a forthcoming sewing book for Chronicle. She is coauthor of *Felt Frenzy* and *AlterNation*, editor of *Just Socks* and *Just Gifts*, and a columnist for knit.1 magazine, as well as a frequent contributor to *CRAFT*, *Yarn Market News*, and *Adorn* magazines. Shannon coordinates the Cleveland edition of indie craft show Bazaar Bizarre, runs an online shop called anezka handmade, and calls Cleveland home.

Alison Stewart-Guinee is the mother of two teen knitters (and a younger son who is a teen wannabe). She spends her summers working with teens as the head of the craft program at a camp in the Colorado Rockies. Alison learned to knit in her teens and loves introducing the teens in her life to the joys of working with sticks and string. When not knitting or teaching knitting, she weaves a line of art-to-wear scarves, bakes wedding cakes, and travels (with teens and knitting in tow, of course). Currently she is working on a line of fanciful knits for intrepid knitters.

Index

find your style online

If your style is grunge, you're probably pretty anti-fashion. But even sweatshirts, flannel shirts, and messenger bags comprise a style. We didn't have room in this book for a chapter on grunge knits, but we didn't want to leave out you lovers of grunge, so we've posted a bonus chapter on our Web site. Check out www.wiley.com/go/findyourstyle for free access to these three great patterns:

- **Green River Legwarmers (designed by Shannon Okey):** These stylish legwarmers (which you can also wear as detachable bell sleeves if your arms get chilly) and hat are grunge inspired but not grungy. The yarn, a soft soy fiber/wool blend called *Karaoke* from South West Trading Company, is slightly shiny, but the colors are muted—perfect for drawing attention to yourself without drawing attention to yourself, if you know what I mean. Rock on!

- **Green River Hat (designed by Shannon Okey):** Here's a hat to match the Green River leg-warmers. Worked in the round, it has no pesky seams and practically no finishing to fuss with. You work the rib and cable just like you do for the legwarmers, but then you shape the top using evenly spaced decreases—that's what makes that nice swirl pattern at the top. Try knitting this in stripes or solids for a completely different look.

- **Flick of the Wrist Warmers (designed by Sharon Turner):** You can't have too many pairs of wrist warmers. What's fun about these is that you get to drop a stitch and create a run *on purpose*. These wrist warmers have a little open-ended thumb covering, which is probably the most challenging part of making this fast and easy accessory. Add 12 or so inches to the length, and you have a chic pair of arm warmers. (Just be sure to buy a couple extra balls of yarn!)